LITTLE FIXES

54 Clever Ways to Extend the Life of Kids' Clothes

reuse • recycle • repurpose • restyle

DISNEY POWLESS

stashBOOKS.

an imprint of C&T Publishing

Dedication

To my Creator

Text copyright © 2014 by Disney Powless

Photography and Artwork copyright © 2014 by C&T Publishing, Inc.

Publisher: Amy Marson

Creative Director: Gailen Runge

Art Director: Kristy Zacharias

Editor: S. Michele Fry

Technical Editors: Doreen Hazel and Gailen Runge

Cover/Book Designer: April Mostek

Page Layout Artist: Kristy Zacharias

Production Coordinator: Jenny Davis

Production Editor: Joanna Burgarino

Illustrator: Jenny Davis

Photo Assistant: Mary Peyton Peppo

Photography by Disney Powless, unless otherwise noted

Published by Stash Books, an imprint of C&T Publishing, Inc., P.O. Box 1456, Lafayette, CA 94549

Library of Congress Cataloging-in-Publication Data

Powless, Disney, 1985-

Little fixes : 54 clever ways to extend the life of kids' clothes - reuse, recycle, repurpose, restyle / Disney Powless.

   pages cm

ISBN 978-1-60705-854-0 (soft cover)

1. Children's clothing. 2. Clothing and dress--Remaking. 3. Clothing and dress--Repairing. I. Title.

TT635.P69 2014

646.4'06--dc23

                              2013043254

Printed in China

10 9 8 7 6 5 4 3 2 1

CONTENTS

Introduction

Spaghetti strikes fear in my heart.

It must be because my daughter has always had an amazing sixth sense that allows her to know as soon as she enters a room what items or activities will ruin her clothing.

As parents and grandparents we know that with red sauce, an active lifestyle, and our kids' unpredictable growth patterns, it's tough to keep a handle on their wardrobes. No sooner is a dress bought than it has stains on it, or a few games of "horsey" and the knees of his new jeans are worn halfway through. Then there is that darling sweater you bought on clearance … but fit perfectly the next July!

So what to do when a delicate dress meets delicious dressing? Don't throw it out! With some basic sewing skills and a little imagination you can find countless ways to make kids' clothing last a little longer. Sometimes it's as easy as stitching a fabric flower over a stain. Other times it may mean adding a few inches of a great plaid flannel to the cuffs of a pair of pants. You'll find yourself getting carried away in the fun of refashioning! And not only will your kids thank you, your wallet will too.

HOW TO USE
THIS BOOK

To help you solve your child's wardrobe issues quickly and easily, I've organized the projects in this book by common problems: ill-fitting clothes, stained or ripped clothes, clothes that fit during the wrong season, and clothes that are seemingly unusable. Many of the fixes can be used for boys or girls, so think outside the box! Then mix and match the patterns (pages 156–158) for endless creative expression.

As you get ready to jump in and start a project, keep an open mind about selecting materials. I use almost entirely recycled fabrics and notions in my sewing, and I love the unique flavor it lends to my projects. Need flannel for a project? Use a man's old shirt! Need a lot of fabric for a ruffled skirt? Try a gorgeous vintage floral sheet. I even love to salvage colored elastic from thrift store suspenders or stretchy belts.

With this book you'll have tons of alteration ideas at your fingertips, but don't let it stop there! Your mind is a great resource, so put it to use and get creative. You never know—you might find a few fixes for your own wardrobe as well!

What about Donating?

With all this talk about saving our kids' clothing from the "donate" pile, I definitely want to say that I am a huge fan of donating. After all, part of the joy in receiving our blessings in life is the opportunity to share them with others. But altering your kids' clothing does not mean you can't donate them to others when you're through with them the second time. In fact, you may find that you're donating something that is even cuter than before. To donate your child's clothing, check your local area for donation sites or contact one of these great service organizations:

Orphan's Lifeline International ◆ *orphanslifeline.org*

Big Brothers Big Sisters ◆ *bbbs.org*

American Red Cross ◆ *redcross.org*

Goodwill Industries ◆ *goodwill.org*

MEET THE
MODELS

I love sewing, but I'm not going to lie: The absolute best part about writing this book was getting to work with these cute little faces! My camera could never capture all the joy, sweetness, and fun of their spirits. I know you'll love them as I do. Let me introduce you!

Elijah
Age: 2
Favorite food:
Salad

Brooklyn
Age: 3
Favorite color:
Red

Skylar
Age: 3
Favorite thing
ever: T. rex

Jack
Age: 4
Favorite person:
Spider-Man

Paige
Age: 5
Favorite animal:
Horse

Brayden
Age: 6
Favorite super
power: Flying

Kayla

Age: 7
Favorite person:
My family

Lexi

Age: 7
Favorite thing
to wear:
Fancy dresses

Dylan

Age: 8
Favorite word:
Awesome

Sarah

Age: 8
Favorite color:
Aquamarine

Tyler

Age: 12
Favorite thing to do
before bedtime:
Wrestle with Dad

Alyssa

Age: 14
Favorite color:
Lavender

SUPPLIES

For the projects in this book you'll need basic sewing supplies such as a sewing machine, needles, thread, sewing pins, an iron, and fabric shears or a rotary cutter and cutting mat.

Other tools and supplies you will need for some of the projects are the following:

Paint (use only a nontoxic paint appropriate for clothing, such as acrylic paint), paintbrushes, a hair dryer, embroidery thread, buttons, elastic, elastic thread, a hot glue gun, large safety pins, clear packing tape, ribbon, snap closures, beads, decorative trim, hook-and-loop fastener, household bleach, fabric and fabric scraps, D-ring belt loops, and hair clips.

For freezer-paper stenciling (page 15) you will need a craft knife and a roll of plastic-coated freezer paper. Freezer paper is available in most grocery stores, or you can check Resources (page 159) for other sources.

For appliqué (page 14) you will need paper-backed fusible web as well as freezer paper.

An optional tool that I find useful is wash-away stitch stabilizer. It's great for preventing knit fabric from stretching while being sewn. Check Resources (page 159) for information on where to buy it.

 Thread

 Scissors

 Pins

 Buttons

 Measuring tape

 Paint

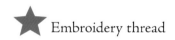 Embroidery thread

TECHNIQUES

The projects in this book are delightfully simple and involve common sewing techniques that you may be familiar with already. For those who are new to sewing (welcome!), I've put together a few step-by-step instructions for the methods you will be using throughout this book. To ensure success with your projects, be sure to read through this chapter before you begin.

Unless otherwise specified, all of the projects use ½″ seams.

Sewing with Knits

T-shirt knits are stretchy, comfortable, and easy to care for, which makes them a great choice for children's clothing. Knits don't unravel, so they often don't even need hemming (which, I'll be honest, is the real reason I love them). However, because of their stretchiness, they may take a little getting used to when you first start working with them. Keep these key points in mind when sewing with knits.

DO: Avoid bunching. **A**

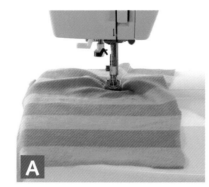

Keep a close eye on your fabric as you sew. If you notice the fabric beginning to bunch in front of the needle, stop sewing, position your needle down in the fabric, and lift the presser foot. Gently smooth out the fabric, lower the presser foot, and continue sewing. With some garments it may be necessary to smooth out bunching fairly often. Be patient and take your time to get the best results. Another option is to use your machine's walking foot, which is designed to sew two layers of fabric together evenly.

DO: Check the tension on your sewing machine. Sometimes it can help to loosen the tension slightly when working with knits. (See your machine's manual for instructions on adjusting tension.) Stitches should lie flat with no pulling (tension too tight) or looping (tension too loose) on either the front or back sides.

DO: Use a ballpoint or stretch needle if you can. While I often skip this step (usually because I'm working between spelling worksheets and tea parties), using the correct needle for your fabric will prevent any snagging and can make your project go a lot more smoothly.

DO: Try wash-away stabilizer. One trick I've learned for working with extra-stretchy fabrics is to apply a ½″-wide strip of adhesive stabilizer along the edges of both fabrics as I sew them together. It prevents stretching and washes out afterward.

DON'T: Skip the pins. It may be tempting to save time by not pinning your fabric, but with a stretchy fabric pinning is essential. The more pins you use, the less your fabric will shift when you sew, so pin well.

DON'T: Pull the fabric.

Unless otherwise noted, it is important to avoid letting your fabric stretch at all while sewing. As you guide the fabric along with your hands, use a light touch and allow the fabric to move freely.

Sewing a Ruffle

Hands down, my favorite accent is the ruffle. I always say everything looks better with a ruffle on it! Luckily, ruffles are as easy to sew as they are to look at.

1. Begin by setting your machine's stitch length to the longest setting and the tension to the highest setting. Sew a continuous row of stitching along the edge of the fabric that you want ruffled. (Note: With lightweight fabrics, these steps alone may ruffle your fabric automatically, especially if you are using an older machine.) Do not backstitch at the beginning or end of the stitching, and leave several inches of thread at each end. Sew an identical row of stitching parallel to the first row, about ⅜" away.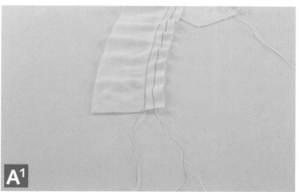

2. Grasp the bobbin threads and gently scoot the fabric downward with your other hand until the ruffles are the desired length. Don't pull the threads too firmly or the stitches may break; then you'll have to start all over. Even out the ruffles by hand.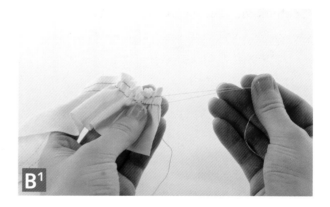

> **NOTE** In some cases you can ruffle using only one row of stitching instead of two. However, if you are working with a heavyweight fabric, one row of stitching may break easily.

Hand Stitching

I like to work fast and furiously, but once in a while I love to sit down with a needle and thread and let my thoughts wander while working on a hand-stitching project. Hand stitching is simple to do and can be a relaxing way to sew.

1. Begin with a generous length of thread in a color that matches the fabric. Wet an end of the thread and push it through the eye of your needle. **A**

2. Pull it through until it is slightly shorter than the other end. Tie a knot in the longer end.

3. Starting on the back of the fabric (to hide the knot), bring the needle up and down through the fabric. **B**

4. When you are done stitching, bring the needle through to the back of the fabric and loop the thread to begin tying a knot. Before pulling the knot tight, insert the needle through the loop and then down into the fabric. **C**

5. Pull the thread until the knot has slid to the bottom of the needle. Snip the thread.

Slip stitch

A slip stitch (sometimes called an invisible stitch or ladder stitch) hides the thread inside the fold of the seam, which makes it a great choice for projects that require closing up a seam from the outside without any stitches showing.

1. Thread your needle and tie a knot in the end. With the edges of the fabric folded toward each other and pinned, insert the needle into the corner and bring it upward, tucking the knot below.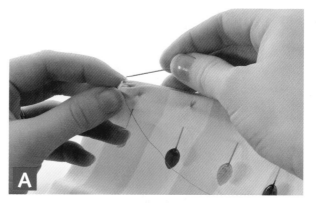

2. Insert the needle into a single layer of the left side of the fabric, coming out about ⅛″ away.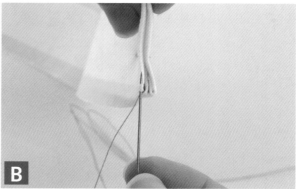

3. Then insert the needle directly across from where you came out into a single layer of the right side, coming out ⅛″ away.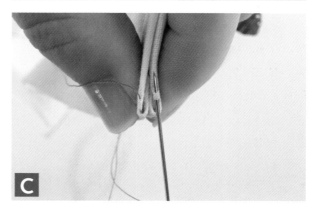

4. Repeat the stitches until you have sewn up the opening. Knot the thread at the bottom and snip the thread. Tuck the knot into the seam.

Appliqué

Appliqué is simply the art of adding one piece of fabric (usually a small shape or design) on top of another fabric. It's a great way to add personality and uniqueness to a project. You can attach the appliqué by simply machine stitching around the edges, or you can use the iron-on method.

The iron-on method of appliqué:

1. Trace your pattern onto the paper side of a piece of paper-backed fusible web. Then cut it out, leaving 1″–2″ around the edges. **A**

2. Place the template onto the *back* of the desired fabric with the paper side up, and iron on according to the manufacturer's instructions. **B**

3. Cut out the appliqué on the lines and peel off the paper backing. **C**

4. Iron the appliqué to the right side of the garment with the adhesive side down. Use a straight stitch, a satin stitch, a zigzag stitch with a decreased stitch length, or a decorative stitch to finish the edges of the appliqué.

TIPS

- When using the iron-on method, remember that your design will be backward when you cut it out. If you are appliquéing letters or other directionally sensitive designs, reverse each design before tracing it onto the paper-backed fusible web.

- Use a piece of freezer paper (shiny side down), silicone pressing sheet, or silicone release paper between your iron and the appliqué to protect the iron from the fusible web. This will keep your iron free of bits of sticky adhesive!

Freezer-Paper Stenciling

A favorite technique of many refashioners (including me) is using plastic-coated freezer paper as an adhesive stencil for painting on clothing. Because you can print on freezer paper, the design possibilities are almost endless!

1. Trace your pattern onto the dull side of a piece of freezer paper with at least 2″ of paper around the edges. **A**

2. Use a craft knife to cut out the design. It's important to keep at least 2″ of paper around your design to keep paint from going onto areas of the garment you *don't* want painted. **B**

3. Place the stencil (shiny side down) onto the garment so that the design is exactly where you want it. Press with a dry iron (no steam) at medium heat for about 45 seconds, checking frequently to avoid burning. **C**

4. When the stencil is firmly in place, slide a piece of heavy paper under the layer you're painting. This will keep the paint from bleeding through to the fabric underneath. Paint over the stencil with acrylic paint. **D**

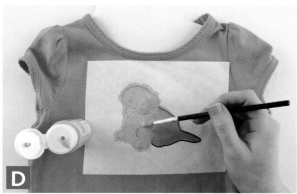

To set the paint:

Let the paint dry completely (about an hour), or dry with a hair dryer. Add additional coats of paint, drying after each layer, until no fabric shows through. After the final coat is dry, cover the design with a lightweight cloth and dry iron over it. Wash painted garments on gentle cycle and lay flat to dry. Iron on the wrong side of the fabric.

Shirring

Shirring is adorable on little girls' clothing, and although it looks complicated, it's actually one of the easiest sewing techniques out there. Try it—I know you'll love it!

1. Wrap elastic thread around your bobbin, stretching the thread slightly as you wind.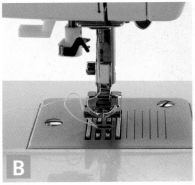

2. If the machine has a drop-in bobbin, use the bobbin winder to wind the elastic thread. Insert the bobbin into the bobbin case and bring up the thread as usual.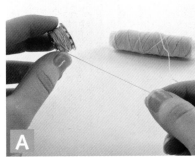

3. Use regular thread as the needle thread in your machine. Sew parallel lines onto the fabric, about ⅝" apart. The fabric will gather slightly as you stitch.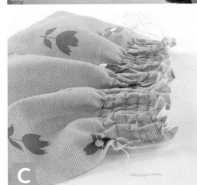

4. It may help to mark out the lines ahead of time with a disappearing-ink pen, or use the edge of your presser foot as a guide for the width of the rows. After you have sewn the desired number of rows, mist the fabric lightly with water.

5. Now iron over the rows of stitching. The heat will cause the elastic to retract, tightening up the gathers.

Turning a Fabric Tube

Some of the projects in this book involve sewing a strip of fabric into a tube. The first step is to fold a long strip of fabric in half lengthwise, with right sides together. Then sew a seam along the raw edge of the folded strip. To make it easier to turn the "tube" right side out, attach a safety pin (as large a pin as will fit through the tube) to one end of the tube. Tuck the pin into the tube and scoot it through until you can pull it out the other side. As you continue to pull on the safety pin, it will draw the fabric and pull the entire length right side out.

WRONG SIZE

No matter how well we take care of our children's clothes, we can't keep them from getting too small, or even too large, in the wrong areas. But with some creativity, sizing issues can be fixed in many ways, all with few or no extra materials. Whether your sweet pumpkins are tall and skinny or short and chubby-cheeked, here are some great ideas for customizing their clothing to the shape and size that fits them.

You'll Need ...

Too-short shirt

Coordinating fabric (½–1 yard)

BEFORE

AFTER

Shirt to Dress

My daughter's shirts have always gotten too short before they got too small. As much as I love to pinch her cute little belly when it shows, I felt triumphant when I found creative ways to fix her shirt-length issues. My favorite is this comfy and cute shirred shirtdress.

1. Cut the shirt off 1″ below your child's waist level and measure around the bottom.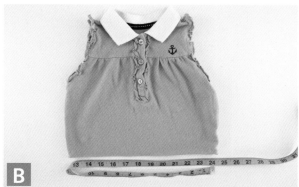

2. Cut a rectangle of fabric for the skirt piece. The length should be twice the measurement from Step 1, plus 1″. The width of the rectangle should be the desired finished dress length plus 4″.

3. Bring the sides of the skirt piece together with right sides facing, and sew.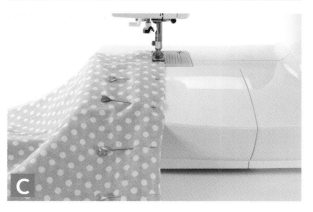

4. Hem the top edge of the skirt piece with a ½″ double-fold hem and the bottom edge with a 1″ double-fold hem.

5. Starting about ¾″ from the top edge, shirr 4 rows at the top of the skirt piece using the shirring technique (page 16).

6. Pin the skirt piece to the bottom of the shirt with a 1″ overlap and sew on using another row of shirring.

TIP For an even easier option, use a preruffled knit fabric like the one I used for Kayla's version (see photograph below). I also added a few inches of the fabric to the neckline as an accent.

TIP Cover an unwanted design on the shirt by adding a quick fabric rosette. Cut a 4″ × 20″ strip of fabric and fold it in half lengthwise with the wrong sides facing each other. Ruffle the raw edges using the ruffling technique (see Sewing a Ruffle, page 11). Then roll into a flower shape starting at the center. Secure the bottom with hand stitching and then hand stitch to the shirt.

OTHER FIX-IT OPTIONS

- Color Block Shirt (page 21)
- Baby Bodysuit to Layered T (page 68)

Paige, *what job would you least like to have when you grow up? "Canning lobster."*

Color Block Shirt

Giving a shirt a color block look is a great way to add length for a boy or girl. Add a graphic with freezer-paper stenciling (page 15) for extra cuteness!

1. Decide where you want the block of color and cut the shirt into 2 pieces there. If you're working with a long-sleeved shirt, be sure the arms and middle section line up nicely.

2. Cut 2 identical rectangles from the coordinating knit fabric. The long side of each rectangle equals the shirtfront width plus 1″. The short side equals the desired additional shirt length plus 1″.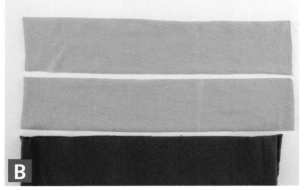

3. Sew the rectangles together on the short sides, with right sides facing. Pin and sew one edge of the block to the bottom of the upper part of the shirt, with right sides facing and side seams matching.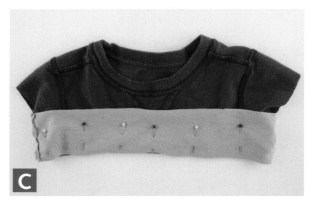

4. Pin and sew the other edge of the block to the lower part of the shirt, with right sides facing and side seams matching.

5. Measure around the sleeve opening. Cut 2 rectangles with long sides equal to the sleeve opening plus 1″. The short side of the rectangle is the same measurement as the short side of the midsection rectangle. **E**

6. Sew each rectangle together on the short sides, to make 2 circles. Pin and sew the sleeve blocks to the sleeves in the same way as the midsection.

7. To add a stenciled graphic, follow the directions for freezer-paper stenciling (page 15). Use any of the patterns (see Patterns, pages 156–158) or design a pattern of your own. **F**

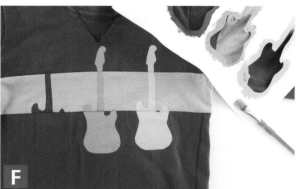

ANOTHER FIX-IT OPTION

- Baby Bodysuit to Layered T (page 68)

Jack, what are you super good at? "Ninja moves."

BEFORE

AFTER

Widen a Shirt

Don't worry if there isn't enough room in the tummy area of those shirts. Adding fabric to the sides is super quick, and it's fun to match up colors and fabrics!

1. Cut the shirt open on both sides along the entire underarm seam, and remove the existing side seams if desired.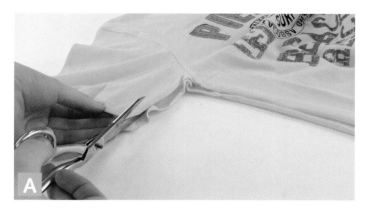

2. Cut 2 side panels. For the length measurement, measure along the entire side seam and add 1″. The width of the side panel should be the desired added width (approximately 1″–4″) plus 1″. Hem both ends of each panel with a ½″ single-fold hem. B

3. Pin a side panel to the back half of the shirt with right sides facing, and sew on. Then pin and sew the other side of the panel to the front half of the shirt with right sides facing. Repeat for the other side of the shirt. C

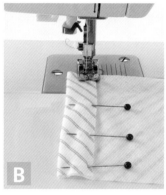

ANOTHER FIX-IT OPTION

- Suspenders Shirt (page 28)

Tyler, what is your favorite holiday? "Thanksgiving."

BEFORE

AFTER

You'll Need ...
Too-big T-shirt

Skinny Shirt

Some brands of shirts run extra wide and never quite fit the more slender kids. Taking in the sides is quick and easy, and then you can use the scraps to personalize the shirt with initials or other shapes. Or save those leftovers for future projects!

1. Have your child try on the shirt, and note the amount to be taken in on each side. Turn the shirt inside out and mark the new side seam lines with a fabric-marking pen. **A**

2. Sew along the marked lines and trim the excess, leaving about ½". **B**

3. Draw your child's initial on the front of the T-shirt with a fabric-marking pen. **C**

4. Use the excess fabric to make your child's initial and pin it on. **D**

5. Sew the initial on with a straight stitch. Add decorative hand stitching with embroidery thread for another custom touch. **E**

TIP Not into letters? Try hearts, geometric shapes, stick figures—anything your mind (or your child's mind!) can imagine.

OTHER FIX-IT OPTIONS

- Tank to Fur Vest (page 104)— try laminated cotton instead of fur

Dylan, why is the grass green? "It helps us play on it."

BEFORE

AFTER

Suspenders Shirt

Add a strip of fabric to each side of a T-shirt to
provide more room for a cute little tummy and
get an adorable "nerdy" suspenders look.

1. Measure from the shoulder seam to the shirt hem.

2. Cut 2 knit suspender pieces with the length equal to twice the measurement from Step 1, plus 3″. The width is 2″–4″, depending on how much you want to add to the shirt. Hem both ends of each strip to match the hemline of the shirt.

3. Cut the shirt through the middle at the shoulder seam on both sides.

4. With right sides facing, pin and sew the side of a strip to the side of the shirt's center section.

5. Sew the other side of the strip to the shirt piece with the sleeve.

6. Repeat Steps 4 and 5 to complete the other side of the shirt.

7. *Optional*: Cut a piece of ribbon long enough to go across the suspenders, plus 1″. Turn under the ends and stitch it onto the shirt. Paint on the pen-in-pocket design (see Patterns, page 156) using the instructions for freezer-paper stenciling (page 15).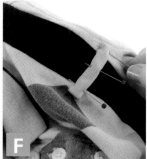

ANOTHER FIX-IT OPTION

- Widen a Shirt (page 24)

Skylar, *what is your favorite color?* "Orange."

You'll Need ...

Too-short pants

Flannel fabric

BEFORE

AFTER

Newly Cuffed Pants

Take pants from high water to high fashion with a cool plaid cuff. Make it fun by using trendy fabrics, or keep it classic with denim-on-denim.

1. Cut off the bottom of each pant leg ½" above the hem stitching.  **A**

2. Measure around the bottom of each leg opening. Cut 2 rectangles of flannel with the length equal to the leg opening plus 1". The width of the rectangles is twice the length you want to add to the pants, plus 1". **B**

3. Sew the ends of a rectangle together with right sides facing. Repeat for the other rectangle. **C**

4. Pin the edge of a flannel cuff to a pants hem piece, with right sides facing and side seams matched. Stitch together, keeping your needle as close to the hemline stitching as possible. **D**

5. *With right sides facing up,* pin and sew the other edge of the flannel cuff to the leg opening. Be sure to match up the side seams! **E**

6. Fold up the cuff halfway and machine stitch along the top to keep the cuff in place. **F**

7. Repeat Steps 4–6 for the other leg.

OTHER FIX-IT OPTIONS

- Pants to Cargo Shorts (page 33)

- Pants to Cut-Offs— Three Ways (page 41)

- Pants to Ruffled Skirt (page 38)

- Roll up long pants into capris (Restyling Ideas, page 129)

Skylar, *who is your favorite person? "Uncle Gavin."*

BEFORE

AFTER

Pants to Cargo Shorts

Are his pants showing a little ankle these days? Or are they looking a little worn at the bottom? Refashion pants by turning them into a rugged pair of cargo shorts!

1. Cut off the pant legs 2″ below the desired finished length.

2. Fold the leg edges under twice (1″ per fold) and hem. For a more professional look, sew 2 parallel lines of stitching, the first along the top fold and the other ½″ below. **B**

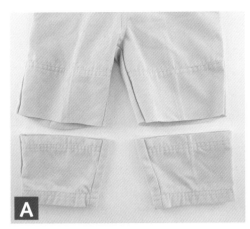

3. Using the pant legs that you removed, cut 2 large squares for pockets, with the hem of the pants as the top edge. Serge or zigzag the sides and bottoms of the new pockets. Then fold over ½″ to the wrong side and press. **C**

4. Center each pocket on the side of a leg. Pin and sew on, leaving the top open. **D**

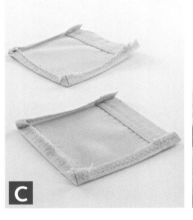

OTHER FIX-IT OPTIONS

- Pants to Cut-Offs—Three Ways (page 41)

- Newly Cuffed Pants (page 30)

- Roll up long pants into capris (Restyling Ideas, page 129)

Elijah, *what word do you use the most? "Mom."*

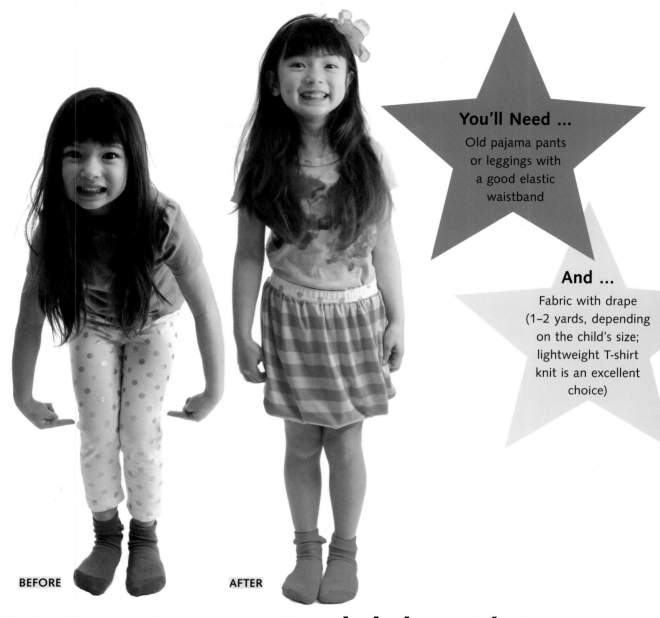

BEFORE

AFTER

You'll Need ...
Old pajama pants or leggings with a good elastic waistband

And ...
Fabric with drape (1–2 yards, depending on the child's size; lightweight T-shirt knit is an excellent choice)

PJ Pants to Bubble Skirt

I remember when I bought my daughter these adorable leggings with gold polka dots. I also remember that the knees were completely worn out in about two days. If your daughter's clothes have worn-out knees—or maybe she has pajama pants that are missing a top—this bubble skirt project is the perfect way to recycle them!

1. Cut off the pant legs just above the inseam.  **A**

2. Measure from the waistband of the pants down to the desired finished length of the skirt and then back up to where you cut off the pants. Add 1½″ for seam allowances. **B**

3. Cut a rectangle for the skirt piece. One side of the rectangle (the skirt length) should equal the measurement calculated in Step 2. The other side of the rectangle (the skirt width) equals twice your child's waist measurement. For the skirt to hang nicely, the length should be on the vertical grainline of the fabric.

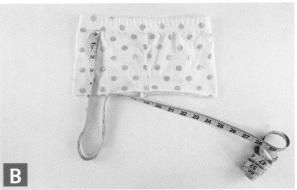

4. Sew the ends of the rectangle together, with right sides facing, to make the skirt piece. Gather the top using the ruffling technique (see Sewing a Ruffle, page 11). **C**

5. Turn the pants inside out. Pin the gathered edge of the skirt piece evenly to the waistband, right sides facing (the skirt piece will be upside down). The gathered stitching line should be just below the elastic waistband of the pants. Be sure to match the skirt seam with the center back seam of the shorts. **D**

6. Sew on with a zigzag stitch and then pull out the gathering stitches.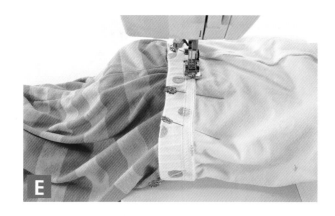

7. Gather the bottom of the skirt and pin to the bottom of the pants with right sides facing up. Rather than matching the skirt's seam with the pants' seam, shift the bottom of the skirt over a few inches before pinning to give it a billowy look. **F**

8. Sew on with a zigzag stitch. **G**

OTHER FIX-IT OPTIONS

- Shorts to Lounge Pants (page 124)

- Shorts to Skort (page 127)

- T-Shirt Headband (page 130)

Paige, *how many people are in the world?* "700."

PANTS: PJ Pants to Bubble Skirt

BEFORE

AFTER

You'll Need ...

Too-short pants

Coordinating knit or
woven cotton fabric
(1–2 yards)

Pants to Ruffled Skirt

When those pants get too short, cut them off and make a
great ruffled skirt! You can get your little one involved by
letting her choose the fabric to add. Try all one fabric or a
rainbow of colors.

1. Cut off the pant legs directly above the inseam. Measure the pants opening all around.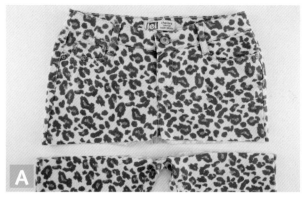

2. To make the base for attaching the ruffles, cut a rectangle with the length equal to the pants opening plus 1″. The width of the rectangle is 5″–10″, depending on the desired finished skirt length.

3. Sew the short ends of the fabric piece together, right sides facing, to make a circle. Then sew a ½″ single-fold hem on an edge.

4. Sew the unhemmed edge of the skirt piece to the bottom of the pants piece with right sides facing. Match the skirt seam to the center back of the pants.

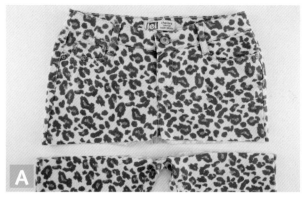

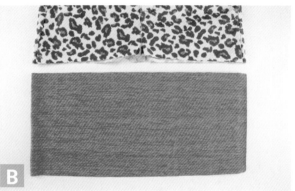

5. Cut 4 strips of fabric, each with a length that is double the width of the skirt piece and a width of 4″ wide. Gather the top edge using the ruffling technique (see Sewing a Ruffle, page 11). If your fabric frays easily, cut the strips 5″ wide and stitch a ½″ hem on the top and bottom of each strip before gathering. **E**

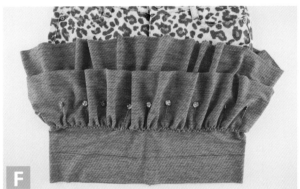

6. Draw lines with a fabric-marking pen to divide the skirt piece into thirds, and then pin and sew the rows of ruffles on the lines. The ruffles will be upside down with right sides facing as you sew. The fourth ruffle is attached to the bottom edge of the skirt piece. **F**

OTHER FIX-IT OPTIONS

- Newly Cuffed Pants (page 30)

- Pants to Cut-Offs—Three Ways (page 41)

Sarah, *what do you wish your mom didn't make you do? "Fold laundry."*

BEFORE

AFTER

You'll Need ...
Too-short pants
or jeans

Pants to Cut-Offs—
Three Ways

This is what I think of as the original clothing refashion: cut-off jeans. Here are three quick ways to turn too-short pants into shorts or capris.

Option 1: Capris

1. Cut off the pant legs just below knee level (or whatever length suits your child).

2. Zigzag stitch about ¾" above the raw edge on each pant leg.

3. Snip the edges about ½" up, being sure not to cut the stitches. Machine wash and dry to get a nice frayed edge.

4. Use the freezer-paper stenciling technique (page 15) to add the whale graphic (see Patterns, page 157).

Option 2: Super-Easy Shorts

1. Cut off the pant legs about 2"–4" (depending on the size of the shorts) below the desired finished hemline.

2. Fold under 1" to the wrong side of the pant legs and iron flat.

3. Fold under again to the desired finished length and sew 2 rows of straight stitches, about ½" apart.

Option 3:
X Marks the Spot

1. Cut off the pant legs about 2″–4″ (depending on the size of the shorts) below the desired finished hemline.

2. Fold up 1″ to the right side of the pant legs and iron flat.

3. Fold up again to the desired finished length. Use embroidery thread to stitch X's around the top of the cuffs.

OTHER FIX-IT OPTIONS

- Pants to Cargo Shorts (page 33)
- Newly Cuffed Pants (page 30)
- Pants to Ruffled Skirt (page 38)

Skylar, *if you were an animal, you'd be: "T. rex."*

DRESSES AND SKIRTS

Skirt 1: Simple Elastic Casing

You'll Need ...

Too-small dress

1"- or 2"-wide elastic

BEFORE

AFTER

Dress to Skirt—Three Ways

My daughter is heartbroken when she has to let go of a dress. Turning it into a skirt is a great way to ease the pain. She loves holding onto a favorite a little longer, and I love how quick and simple this remedy is!

1. To find out how much elastic you need for the waistband, measure around your child's waist, comfortably but with no slack, and add 1″. Cut a piece of elastic to that length.

2. Cut off the dress just below the bodice. Then fold over the top edge of the skirt section ¼″ and baste in place.

3. Fold the basted edge down (wrong sides facing) over the length of elastic, and pin all the way around the skirt piece.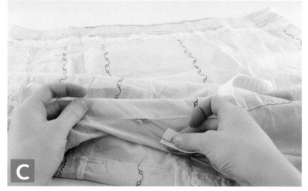

4. Remove the elastic and sew most of the way around, leaving a 1″ opening at the back of the skirt. Pull out the basting stitches. B

5. Pin a large safety pin in an end of the elastic and hold onto it while gently scooting the elastic through the casing. C

6. When the elastic is through the casing, overlap the ends by 1″, and sew back and forth several times with a zigzag stitch. Slide the elastic back into the casing. D

7. Return to the straight-stitch setting and sew the 1″ opening in the casing closed. Be careful not to sew over the elastic. E

Skirt 2: Exposed elastic

You'll Need ...

Too-small dress

1″- or 2″-wide patterned elastic

BEFORE

AFTER

1. To find out how much elastic you need for the waistband, measure around your child's waist, comfortably but with no slack, and add 1". Cut a piece of elastic to that length.

2. Cut off the dress just below the waist level or just below the waistline seam. If the fabric frays easily, serge or zigzag stitch the raw edge.

3. Pin the 2 ends of the elastic together, right sides facing, to create a waistband. Try the waistband on to make sure it's a good fit. Sew together.

4. Gather the top of the skirt piece, using the ruffling technique (see Sewing a Ruffle, page 11), until it is just a few inches wider than the waistband.

5. Pin the elastic waistband to the skirt piece evenly, with right sides facing and edges flush. Be sure the waistband seam matches the center back seam of the skirt.

6. Sew on with a narrow zigzag stitch, gently stretching the elastic as you sew to match the length of the skirt piece.

Skirt 3: Button-Back

You'll Need ...

Too-small dress

Snaps or hook-and-eye closures

BEFORE

AFTER

1. On a dress with a button-up back, cut off the bodice about 2″ above the bottom button.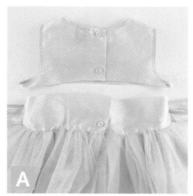

2. Turn the raw edge of the skirt waistband under ¼″ and press. Turn under another ¼″ and sew. You can turn under a little more to make the waistband narrower if desired. **B**

3. Hand stitch a snap or hook-and-eye fastener to the top of the waistband for extra closure reinforcement. **C**

TIP Because this dress was too short for your little girl, the waistband will probably be small enough to stay up on its own. However, if needed, you can sew a ribbon to each side of the skirt's waistband and tie the ribbons in the back.

OTHER FIX-IT OPTIONS

- Easy-On Infinity Scarf (page 150)
- Covered Bead Necklace (page 138)

Paige, *what do you want for your next birthday? "Glitter!"*

BEFORE

AFTER

You'll Need ...
Too-short dress

Dress to Tunic

We all know about adding fabric to make short dresses longer. But have you ever thought of cutting length *off*? This makes a sweet little tunic instead of an "Is-it-a-dress?-Is-it-a-shirt?" awkward fashion statement. You can even use the extra fabric to make a bow or flower. Ahhh, now we've got a fashion statement!

1. Cut the hem off the dress about 1″ above the hem stitching line.

2. Measure and mark an appropriate tunic length for your child. Trim the dress below the marking, making sure it's even all around. Save the extra fabric to make a matching bow (page 52).

3. Trim the hem piece so that it matches the new width of the tunic bottom plus 1″ for a seam allowance. Then resew the side seam with right sides facing.

4. Pin the hem piece upside down to the tunic bottom, with right sides facing and raw edges even.

5. Sew on. Try using the stabilizer technique (see Sewing with Knits, page 10) between the layers to prevent stretching.

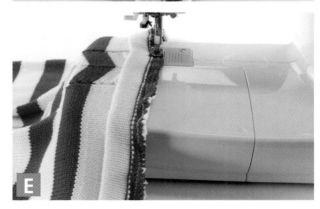

The Bow

1. Determine the size bow you'd like. From the extra fabric, cut 2 rectangles a little larger than the desired bow size. Lay them together with right sides facing and sew along 3 sides. Turn right side out and slipstitch (page 13) the opening closed.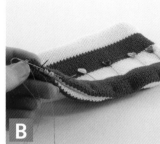

2. Cut a 2″ × 4″ rectangle. Hem all sides if necessary to prevent fraying. Fold the short sides under to meet in the back of the large piece from Step 1. Hand stitch the ends together.

3. Hand stitch the bow to the shoulder seam of the tunic. Or, for a matching accessory, hot glue it to a barrette or headband.

OTHER FIX-IT OPTIONS

- As-Long-as-You-Like Skirt (page 56)
- Dress to Skirt—Three Ways (page 44)

Kayla, what word do you use most? "Love."

BEFORE

AFTER

Overall Overhaul

Even with adjustable straps, overall dresses always get too short too quickly. Replacing the straps is easier than you'd think! Then add a sweet ruffle and you're ready to go!

1. Remove the straps by cutting them off about ½″ from where they are attached to the back of the dress. Remove a strap from its buckle, leaving the other buckle on for now. **A**

2. Trace each side of the strap onto a double layer of fabric, adding ½″ around the sides and 2″ to the top and bottom. Cut out and set aside. Repeat to make another strap set. **B**

3. Pin 2 strap pieces together with right sides facing and sew along 3 edges. Leave open the edge that attaches to the back of the dress. **C**

4. Turn right side out and fold the bottom edges to the inside of the strap. Pin and sew the strap over the area where the original straps were cut off. **D**

5. Thread the strap back through the buckle, using the other strap as a guide, and hand stitch the strap in place. **E**

6. Repeat Steps 3–5 for the other strap.

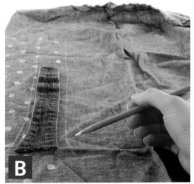

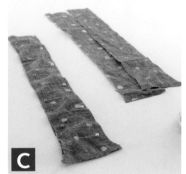

7. Measure around the bottom of the skirt. Cut a strip of fabric with a length equal to 1½ times the length of the dress opening, plus 1″. The width of the strip is the desired added dress length plus 1½″.

8. Sew the short ends together with right sides facing. Sew a ½″ double-fold hem on an edge.

9. Gather the strip (see Sewing a Ruffle, page 11) to match the length of the dress opening. Pin it underneath the dress, with right sides facing up and the gathing stitches hidden under the skirt's hemline. Sew the ruffle on with thread that matches the dress.

10. Paint on matching polka dots or other designs. Follow the paint-setting instructions in Freezer-Paper Stenciling (page 15). For more charm, add a matching bow! **H**

TIP Try making the ruffle out of fun, trendy cottons, or more classic fabrics such as denim or girly chiffon.

OTHER FIX-IT OPTIONS

Brooklyn, *what is your favorite holiday?* "Birthdays."

BEFORE

AFTER

As-Long-as-You-Like Skirt

Does she have a favorite skirt that's gotten too short? Add a layer or two (or even five!) to make it fit and make it fun.

1. Measure around the bottom of the skirt. Cut a layer strip with the length equal to 1½ times the skirt measurement, plus 1″. The width of the layer should be about 3″–5″, depending on your preference and the number of layers you want.

2. Sew the short ends of the strip together with right sides facing to make a circle. B

3. Gather the top of the layer piece, using the ruffling technique (see Sewing a Ruffle, page 11), until it is the same width as the skirt bottom. C

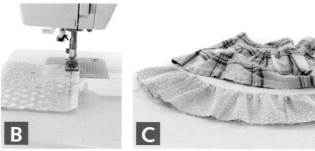

4. Pin and sew the gathered edge to the skirt bottom, with right sides facing. The ruffle should be upside down as you sew. D

5. Repeat Steps 1–4 for additional layers. Hem the last layer. E

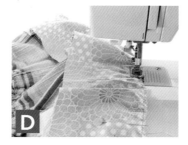

6. *Optional*: Sew 2 large coordinating buttons to the front of the waistband. F

ANOTHER FIX-IT OPTION

- Wear with leggings (Restyling Ideas, page 129)

Lexi, *what job would you least like to have when you grow up? "Putting people in jail, because I'd be sad for them."*

BEFORE   AFTER

You'll Need ...

Too-short jacket

Coordinating
fleece fabric

Suddenly Longer Jacket

Has your child ever grown out of his jacket just a month before
the warm weather arrived? At that point you're more likely to
find him swim trunks than a new jacket, but don't worry! Adding
a bit of fleece is all you need to do to get that too-short jacket
to the end of the season.

1. Measure around the bottom of the jacket. Cut a rectangle with the length equal to the jacket measurement, plus 1″. The width equals twice the desired added jacket length, plus 2″. **A**

2. Fold the rectangle in half lengthwise with right sides facing. Sew up both ends. Turn right side out. **B**

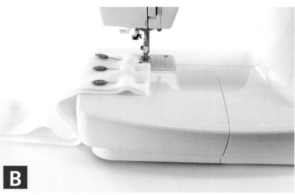

3. Sew along the bottom (folded) edge for a decorative touch. **C**

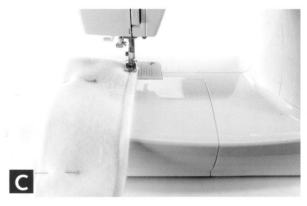

4. Pin and sew the top (unfolded) edge of the fleece strip to the inside of the jacket, right sides facing up. Align the edges of the fleece strip with the edges of the jacket front. Match your stitches to the stitching already on the hemline of the jacket. **D**

5. Measure around the sleeve opening. Cut 2 rectangles with the length equal to the sleeve opening plus 1″. Make the width of each rectangle twice the desired added sleeve length, plus 1″. **E**

6. Sew the ends of each rectangle together with right sides facing to make 2 circles. Then fold in half with wrong sides facing. Follow Steps 3 and 4 to attach the fleece to the sleeve openings. **F**

TIP For a jacket with no front closure, measure halfway around the jacket. Cut 2 rectangles with the length equal to the jacket measurement plus 1″. Make the width equal to twice the desired added jacket length, plus 1″.

Sew the short ends together to make a circle. Follow Steps 3 and 4 to attach the fleece to the bottom of the jacket.

OTHER FIX-IT OPTIONS

- Coat to Cropped Jacket (page 120)
- Cardigan with Ruffles (page 63)

Skylar, *where would you like to go on vacation? "A restaurant."*

BEFORE

AFTER

You'll Need ...
Too-small coat

Coat to Vest

Your kiddo can't wear that puffy coat from two years ago ... or can he? Why not cut off the arms to make a cool puffer vest?

1. Cut off the coat sleeves evenly, leaving about 2″ of fabric beyond the armhole seam.

2. Remove any stitching in the padding in the armhole hem area. **B**

3. Remove any excess insulation from the armhole hem area. **C**

4. Fold the outer fabric and lining under toward each other, getting as close to the shoulder seams as possible. Pin well. **D**

5. Repeat Steps 2–4 for the other armhole. **E**

6. Sew all the way around each armhole.

TIP Follow Steps 1–5 to eliminate the hood if desired.

ANOTHER FIX-IT OPTION

- Suddenly Longer Jacket (page 58)

Brayden, *what is the funniest thing about grownups? "They always laugh at you."*

BEFORE

AFTER

You'll Need ...
Too-short
cardigan

And ...
Coordinating nylon
chiffon or lightweight
cotton fabric
(1 yard)

Cardigan with Ruffles

Adding a row of ruffles can magically turn a plain cardigan
into something sweet and feminine. It also adds just
enough length when those sleeves are getting too short!

1. Measure all around the bottom of the cardigan. Cut a strip of fabric with the length equal to twice the cardigan measurement, plus 1″. The width should be twice the desired added length, plus 1″. **A**

2. Fold the fabric in half lengthwise with right sides facing, and sew up both ends. Turn right side out. **B**

3. Gather the top edge using the ruffling technique (see Sewing a Ruffle, page 11). **C**

4. Pin the ruffled edge to the inside of the bottom of the cardigan, overlapping about ½″, and sew on with a zigzag stitch. **D**

5. Measure the sleeve opening. Cut 2 identical rectangles for the sleeves. The length of the rectangles should be twice the sleeve opening measurement, plus 1″. The width of the rectangles should be twice the desired added length, plus 1″.

6. Sew the short ends of each strip together, with right sides facing, to make 2 circles. Then fold in half lengthwise, with wrong sides facing.

7. Follow Steps 3 and 4 to make a ruffle and attach it to the sleeve. Repeat for the second sleeve.

OTHER FIX-IT OPTIONS

- Shortening Sleeves—Three Ways (page 110)
- Suddenly Longer Jacket (page 58)

Paige, *who do you think should be president? "Me."*

OUTERWEAR: Cardigan with Ruffles **65**

BEFORE

AFTER

You'll Need ...
Pants or skirt
1″-wide elastic
Buttons

Adjustable Waistband

I am convinced that the adjustable waistband is one of the greatest inventions of all time. It's easier than you think to add one yourself.

1. Sew 2 buttons on the inside of the waistband of the pants or skirt, on each side of the zipper opening.  A

2. Cut enough elastic to fit around the waist from button to button. Measure your buttons. Make 5 buttonholes, about ½" apart, in each side of the elastic. B

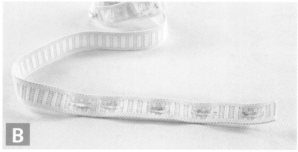

3. Snip a 1" opening in the pants or skirt next to each button. Fold the raw edges under slightly and hand stitch to keep them from fraying. C

4. Attach an end of the elastic to a button. Use a safety pin to guide the other end through the waistband. D

5. Attach the elastic to the button on the other side. E

Dylan, *where would you like to go on vacation? "Seaside, Oregon."*

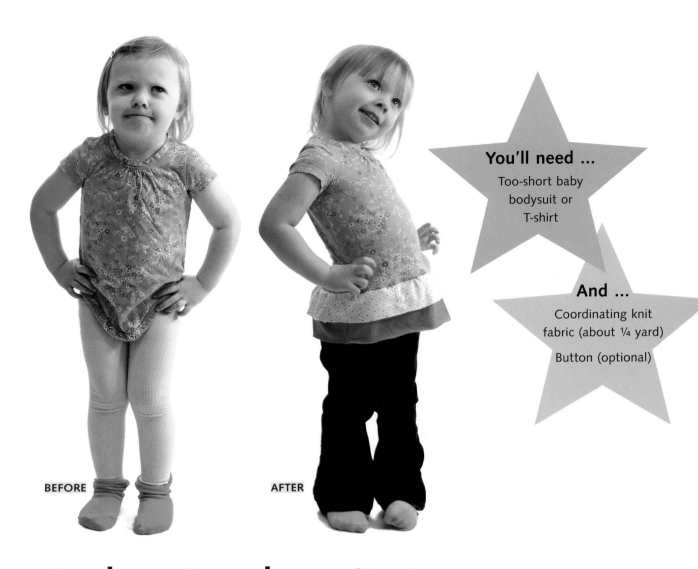

AFTER

You'll need ...

Too-short baby
bodysuit or
T-shirt

And ...

Coordinating knit
fabric (about ¼ yard)

Button (optional)

Baby Bodysuit to Layered T

Most parents are familiar with the "baby bodysuit snap struggle" as I like to call it: pulling and stretching that favorite baby bodysuit, trying to get those snaps to meet across a puffy diaper one more time. Here's a great way to wear it longer without fighting the fasteners!

1. Cut the baby bodysuit straight across, directly above the leg openings. **A**

2. Measure around the bottom of the top piece. Cut 2 strips of knit fabric with a length equal to 1½ times the bodysuit measurement, plus 1″. Make 1 strip about 4″ wide and the other about 2″ wide. **B**

3. Sew the ends of each strip together with right sides facing to make 2 circles. Then gather the top edge of each strip, using the ruffling technique (see Sewing a Ruffle, page 11), until they match the width of the shirt. **C**

4. Spread the gathers evenly on both strips. Baste the 2 ruffles together along the gathered edges.

5. Pin the double ruffle upside down to the bottom of the bodysuit, with right sides facing and side seams matching. **D**

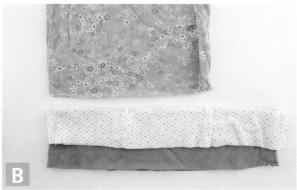

6. Sew it on with a narrow zigzag stitch and then pull out the gathering and basting stitches.

7. For extra pizzazz, stitch on some poppy flowers (see Patterns, page 158) in the same or different fabric.

TIP For a boy version, cut the fabric strip to match the width of the shirt plus a 1″ seam allowance and skip the ruffling step.

Brooklyn, what are you super good at? "Getting myself dressed."

BEFORE

AFTER

You'll Need ...
Too-small tights
½″-wide elastic

Tights to Knee-Highs

Is there anything cuter than a little girl in knee-high stockings? When my daughter was very young, I had a really difficult time finding knee-highs in her size, so I came up with this idea to make my own! It's a great way to repurpose tights that are a size or two too small.

1. Cut off the legs from a pair of tights at the very top.

2. Measure around your child's leg just below the knee. Cut 2 pieces of elastic to that length plus 1".

3. Lay the ends of the elastic on top of each other, overlapping about ½", and sew together. You will have 2 elastic circles.

4. Fold the top 1" of the sock over the elastic and pin.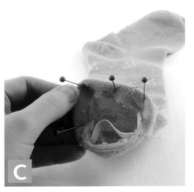

5. Sew, being careful not to sew on the elastic. You may need to stretch the elastic a little as you stitch.

TIP Embellish the stockings by adding bows (page 52), buttons, or ruffles to the top. Or apply paint (see Freezer-Paper Stenciling, page 15).

Brooklyn, *what is your favorite part of the day? "When Daddy comes home."*

ANOTHER FIX-IT OPTION

- T-Shirt Headband (page 130)

STAINS AND RIPS

Kids play hard! It's wonderful, but their clothing usually suffers. For me, that's when the fun starts. Covering stains and rips are some of my favorite projects because, well ... they're easy! Some of the methods are used here specifically for stains or for rips, but they could actually be a fix for either. Let your style and imagination be your guide. This chapter has some great ideas to help you get started.

Many of the techniques presented here will work for revamping ripped items as well.

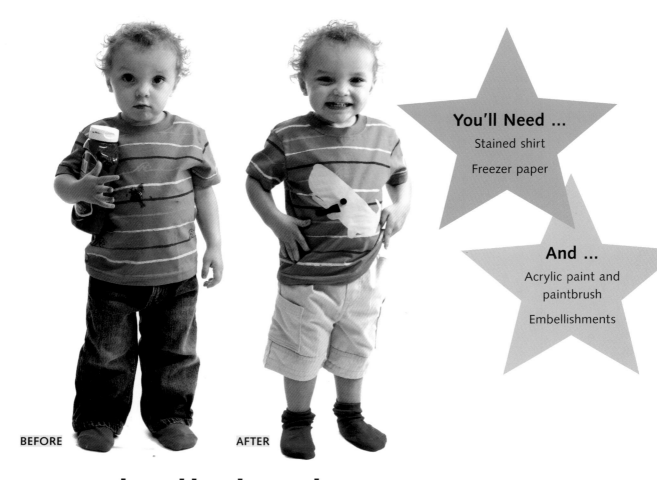

BEFORE

AFTER

You'll Need ...

Stained shirt

Freezer paper

And ...

Acrylic paint and paintbrush

Embellishments

Embellished Freezer-Paper Stenciling

Freezer-paper stenciling (page 15) is lots of fun, but it's even more fun when you add a little three-dimensional flair! Use ribbon, fabric, sequins, patches, or other embellishments. You could even get your little one involved with the design process.

1. Choose a pattern (see Patterns, pages 156–158) and paint the design on using the freezer-paper stenciling technique (page 15).

2. Stitch on a little bow or bow tie for a preppy puppy or a dapper whale. B

3. Add sparkle with sequins—they make great raindrops, eyes, stars, or pearl necklaces. C

4. Gather (see Sewing a Ruffle, page 11) up some scrap fabric to give a puppy a tulle tutu. D

5. Use embroidery thread to stitch detail onto a simple silhouette. Try guitar strings, butterfly wing designs, dalmatian spots, poppy flower stems, or ship masts. **E**

OTHER FIX-IT OPTIONS

- Reverse Appliqué (page 97)

- T-Shirt Transplant (page 92)

- Polka-Dot Sweater Patches (page 90)

Elijah, what is your favorite thing in the world? "Never Land Pirates."

BEFORE

AFTER

Galaxy Shirt

It's happened to all of us—the dreaded bleach
spot. Just go with it and turn the spot into a fun
bleach-stained pattern!

1. Wear old clothing and latex gloves. Fill a spray bottle with bleach and adjust the nozzle halfway between "spray" and "stream."

2. Spray the front and back of the shirt. Start with small squirts and then wait a moment to let the bleach activate. See how it looks before adding more.

3. Use the freezer-paper stenciling technique (page 15) to add small and large star shapes (see Patterns, page 158).

4. Wash and dry the shirt before letting your young one wear it.

OTHER FIX-IT OPTIONS

- Work-of-Art Shirt (page 117)
- Ruffle-Panel Shirt (page 79)
- Butterfly Cutout Shirt (page 83)
- Embellished Freezer-Paper Stenciling (page 74)

Dylan, *what makes you upset? "Doing homework."*

BEFORE

AFTER

Ruffle-Panel Shirt

Use rows of sweet ruffles to hide spots and stains on the front of a shirt. Try rows in all one color or rainbow ruffles!

1. Cut several strips of fabric. The length of each strip should equal about 1½ times the shirt width you want to cover. The width of each strip is 2″–4″, depending on your preference. You'll need enough strips to cover the front of the shirt, with the strips overlapping by half their width. **A**

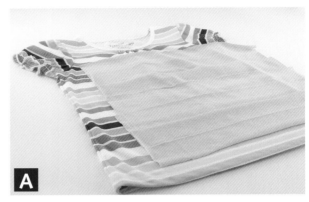

2. Gather each strip using the ruffling technique (see Sewing a Ruffle, page 11). **B**

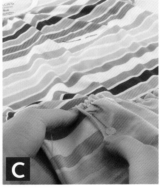

3. Pin the gathered strips to the front of the shirt, starting with the bottom ruffle. Overlap the ruffles by half their width. Be sure the ruffles cover the stain or rip completely. **C**

4. Sew the ruffles to the shirt. **D**

TIP For an even easier version, try cutting out a square or rectangle of preruffled fabric and sewing it to the front of the shirt.

Lexi, *what is the hardest thing you've ever done? "Teach my brother Skylar how to do things."*

OTHER FIX-IT OPTIONS

- T-Shirt Transplant (page 92)
- Work-of-Art Shirt (page 117)
- Embellished Freezer-Paper Stenciling (page 74)

BEFORE

AFTER

You'll Need ...
Stained/discolored tights

And ...
Paper cups or poster board

Acrylic paint and paintbrush

Painted Tights

Cleverly disguise dingy knees with artistic paint swipes for a fun and whimsical look!

1. Push paper cups or rolled-up pieces of poster board into the legs of the tights.

2. Using a dry paintbrush, brush on strokes of paint, covering the stained areas first.

3. Add more strokes in various colors until the tights are covered.

4. Set the paint following the instructions in Freezer-Paper Stenciling (page 15).

TIP Always wash the tights by hand for proper upkeep.

Paige, *what is your favorite color? "Rainbow."*

BEFORE

AFTER

Butterfly Cutout Shirt

Sometimes it's hard to cover stains when they are in more than one place. A kaleidoscope of butterflies fluttering across the front of a shirt is a great way to hide lots of little stains.

1. Trace the butterfly pattern (see Patterns, page 157) onto paper or template plastic, enlarging or reducing it as needed. Cut out the template.

2. Trace the butterflies from the template onto scraps of knit fabric with a fabric-marking pen, and cut them out.

3. Arrange and pin the butterflies on the shirt.

4. Machine or hand stitch 2 lines down the center of each butterfly, allowing the wings to "flap" freely. Use contrasting embroidery thread to accent the centers.

TIP Mix and match patterns, fabrics, and thread colors to suit your child's tastes!

OTHER FIX-IT OPTIONS

- Poppy-Scattered Shirt (page 85)
- Faux Plaid Shirt (page 88)
- Polka-Dot Sweater Patches (page 90)

Kayla, *if you were an animal, you'd be: "A tiger."*

BEFORE

AFTER

Poppy-Scattered Shirt

Is her shirt stained around the neck? Add a row of beautiful poppies right at the neckline! Are there stains in several places? Let the petals scatter across the entire front of the shirt.

1. Trace large, medium, and small poppy patterns (see Patterns, page 158) onto paper or template plastic. Cut out the templates. **A**

2. Trace the poppies from the templates onto the knit fabric with a fabric-marking pen. **B**

3. Cut out a poppy piece of each size per flower and place them on top of each other, with the smallest piece on top. **C**

4. Use a needle and thread to stitch a large X in the middle of each flower. **D**

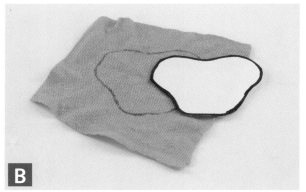

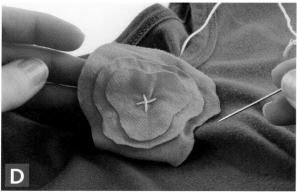

5. Hand or machine stitch the poppy flowers along the neckline, placing them close enough to each other to push the petals up slightly.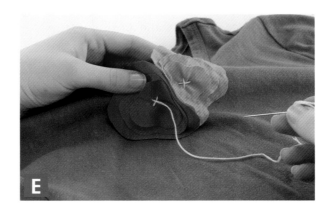

6. If needed, cover other stains by placing flowers in a scattered pattern. **F**

TIP For boys' shirts, try scattering cars, puppies, or simple graphic shapes.

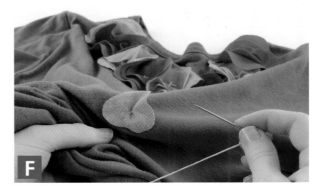

OTHER FIX-IT OPTIONS

- Butterfly Cutout Shirt (page 83)
- Faux Plaid Shirt (page 88)
- Polka-Dot Sweater Patches (page 90)

Alyssa, *what are you super good at?* *"Talking too much."*

STAINS: Poppy-Scattered Shirt **87**

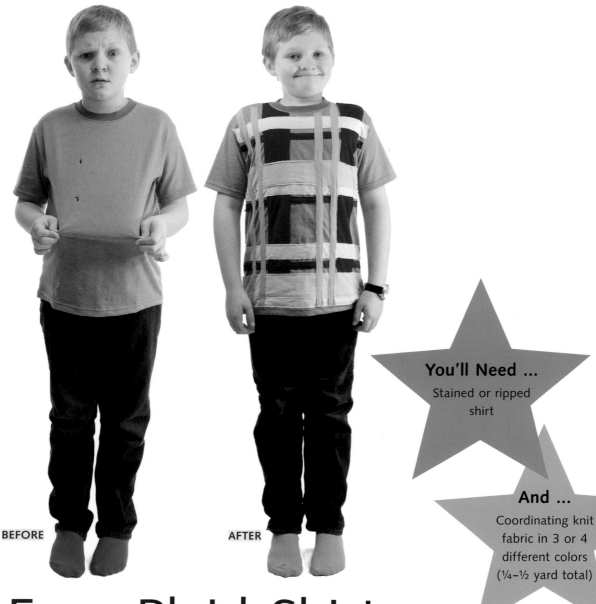

BEFORE

AFTER

Faux Plaid Shirt

A faux plaid design can hide stains in funny places. Really? There's a jelly stain under your arm? This is also a fun way to embellish a shirt even if it doesn't have stains. Just add strips of knit in different colors and directions.

1. Cut 2 wide strips and 4 narrow strips of knit from 2 colors. The length of the strips should equal the length of the shirtfront. **A**

2. Cut 2 wide strips, 4 medium strips, and 3 narrow strips from 3 colors. The length of these strips should equal the width of the shirtfront. **B**

3. Pin and sew the strips down, a strip at a time, in this order: narrow horizontal strips, wide vertical strips, medium horizontal strips, wide horizontal strips, and then narrow vertical strips. **C**

Tyler, what is the funniest thing about grown-ups? "They talk about politics."

OTHER FIX-IT OPTIONS

- Galaxy Shirt (page 77)
- Embellished Freezer-Paper Stenciling (page 74)
- Poppy-Scattered Shirt (page 85)
- Polka-Dot Sweater Patches (page 90)

Many of the ideas in this section can be applied when the problem is a stain as well.

BEFORE

AFTER

You'll Need ...
Sweater with holes

Scraps of knit
fabric

And ...
Paper-backed fusible web

Embroidery
thread

Polka-Dot Sweater Patches

Snags and holes turn up in the weirdest places sometimes. While it might look strange to put one patch on to cover a hole, hiding it with lots of polka-dot patches looks fun and cute!

1. Use the iron-on appliqué technique (page 14) to create 20–30 circle appliqués.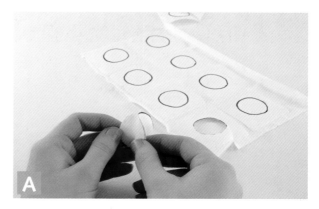

2. Place a dot over each hole and iron the patches on according to the fusible web manufacturer's instructions. Place the other dots all around the sweater and iron on.

3. If desired, hand stitch around the dots with matching embroidery thread.

TIP Try different-colored polka dots, or stitch around the dots with a fun contrasting thread color for a whimsical look.

OTHER FIX-IT OPTIONS

- Arm or Leg Warmers (page 142)
- Poppy-Scattered Shirt (page 85)

Sarah, *what is your favorite sandwich? "Peanut butter and cheese puffs."*

RIPS: Polka-Dot Sweater Patches **91**

BEFORE

AFTER

You'll Need ...
Ripped or stained shirt

And ...
Ill-fitting shirt with a fun design

T-Shirt Transplant

I love how easy this project is! Sewing part of one T-shirt onto another not only covers any stains but is also a great way to recycle a favorite T-shirt that has gotten too small.

1. Measure the length and width of the area on the shirtfront that you want to cover.  **A**

2. Search the "too-small" bin for a T-shirt with a fun design or grab an old adult-sized T-shirt. Mark cutting lines with a fabric-marking pen and a ruler, based on your measurements from Step 1. Cut out the design. **B**

3. Pin the cut-out design to the front of the stained shirt. **C**

4. Sew all the way around the design, close to the edge of your "transplant." Use 2 rows of stitching for a decorative effect. Be careful not to stitch the back of the T-shirt! **D**

OTHER FIX-IT OPTIONS

- Embellished Freezer-Paper Stenciling (page 74)

- Work-of-Art Shirt (page 117)

Skylar, *what is your favorite holiday? "Halloween ... treats."*

BEFORE

AFTER

Knee-Hole Patches

The number one issue that parents face with kids'
clothing has got to be the classic hole in the knee.
Cover a hole with a fun patch or add patches to a
new pair of pants to prevent future holes.

1. Measure the hole you are going to cover.

2. Trace an oval, or the star or heart pattern (see Patterns, page 158), onto paper or template plastic, enlarging the design if necessary to cover the hole well. Cut out the template and set it aside. **B**

3. Cut a piece of denim about 1″ larger than the pattern all around. Cut a piece of fusible web a little smaller than the denim. With the fusible side down and the paper on top, iron the fusible web to the wrong side of the denim. Remove the paper backing. **C**

TIP To protect your iron, use a piece of freezer paper (shiny side down) or silicone release paper between your iron and the paper-backed web.

4. Trace the template onto the *right* side of the fused denim using a fabric-marking pen. **D**

5. Following the traced pattern lines, serge or sew around the edges with a satin stitch (or zigzag stitch with a short stitch length). Trim around the shape close to the stitching. **E**

6. Place a piece of freezer paper inside the pant leg behind the hole, shiny side up (to keep from fusing the patch to the back of the pants!). Iron the patch to the right side of the pant leg, covering the hole, and then hand stitch it on along the edges. **F**

TIPS

- Use colored denim patches for a little pop of whimsy.

- Cut an extra patch in a fun corduroy print and fuse it on top of the denim patch after Step 5.

- Try using knit fabric to add patches to girls' leggings for a cute look!

ANOTHER FIX-IT OPTION

- Pants to Cut-Offs—Three Ways (page 41)

Dylan, *why do your parents love you?*
"Because I am a blessing to them."

BEFORE

AFTER

Reverse Appliqué

Reverse appliqué is just what it sounds like: appliqué in reverse! Add fabric to the *wrong* side of the shirt to turn rips and holes into something decorative.

1. Choose a pattern (see Patterns, pages 156–158) and enlarge or reduce it to the desired size. Trace the design onto paper or template plastic and cut it out. **A**

2. Trace the template design onto the right side of the shirt, making sure to completely cover the hole or tear. **B**

3. Pin a large square of knit fabric to the wrong side of the shirtfront behind the template design. Make sure the knit fabric covers at least 1″ beyond all the edges of the template design. **C**

4. With the right side of the shirt facing up, sew along the marked lines with a satin or zigzag stitch. **D**

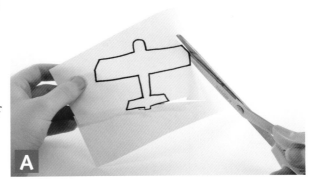

5. Carefully snip away the shirt fabric close to the stitches, revealing the knit fabric underneath. Be careful not to cut the knit fabric appliqué!

6. Turn the shirt over and trim any excess knit, leaving ½" around the stitches.

OTHER FIX-IT OPTIONS

- T-Shirt Transplant (page 92)

- Faux Plaid Shirt (page 88)— try using just a few "stripes"

Elijah, *what are you super good at?* "Tackling."

BEFORE

AFTER

Bib-Front Shirt

There were some times in my daughter's life when I wished she could wear a bib all day, every day, to keep from staining the necklines of her shirts. When the stains won't come out, try replacing the area and turning it into a cute layered-look shirt!

1. Use a fabric-marking pen to trace an oval shape on the front of the damaged shirt and a slightly shorter oval shape on the back. It may help to trace around a platter or other oval-shaped item. The oval should be about ½″ smaller than you want the new shirtfront to be.

2. Carefully cut along the traced lines.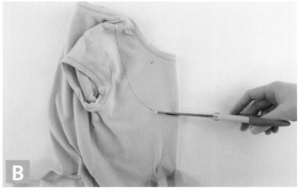

3. Tuck the collared shirt into the stained shirt. Match and pin together at the shoulder seams. Trace the neckline. Cut ½″ outside the line for the new neckline on the front and back of the collared shirt.

4. Turn the stained shirt and the collared shirt piece inside out and pin the raw edges together with right sides facing.

5. Sew all the way around the neckline, being careful not to sew the body of the shirt into the bib seam. 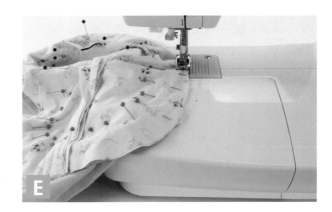 **E**

6. Turn right side out and press the seam toward the bib. **F**

TIP Sew lace or other trim to the edge for extra cuteness. For Kayla's shirt, I used the ruffled trim that was on the bottom of the collared shirt.

ANOTHER FIX-IT OPTION

- Poppy-Scattered Shirt (page 85)

Kayla, *how many times a day do you like to eat? "All day."*

OUT OF SEASON

Have you ever been tempted by a great after-season clearance sale, even though you weren't sure which size your little one would be next year? Or gotten a lovely gift that just never quite fit at the right time? We've all been there. (Groan.) However, with only a few snips and stitches, many times the garment can be made perfectly wearable whenever you need it.

BEFORE

AFTER

Tank to Fur Vest

Have a tank that fits in the wintertime? Use
fleece or faux fur to turn it into a snuggly vest.

1. Cut a line through the middle of the front of the tank, from neckline to hem. Use a plate to mark and cut round edges for the lower front sections. Trim a little off the bottom if desired. **A**

2. Turn the tank inside out and trace the back and both fronts onto paper, adding ½" on all sides. **B**

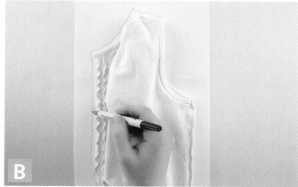

3. Cut out the paper patterns and pin them to the faux fur fabric. Cut out. **C**

4. Pin the front pieces to the back piece at the sides and shoulders, with right sides facing. Sew together. **D**

5. Place the fur vest inside the tank top with the right side of the fur vest facing the wrong side of the tank top. Pin the vest and tank together, leaving the neckline and armholes open. **E**

6. Sew along the pinned edges. **F**

7. Turn right side out. Fold under and pin the fur fabric along the armholes and neckline. Sew along the pinned edges. **G**

8. Sew a 10″ length of ribbon to each side of the front of the vest. **H**

E

F

G

Paige, what word do you use the most? "Mommy."

H

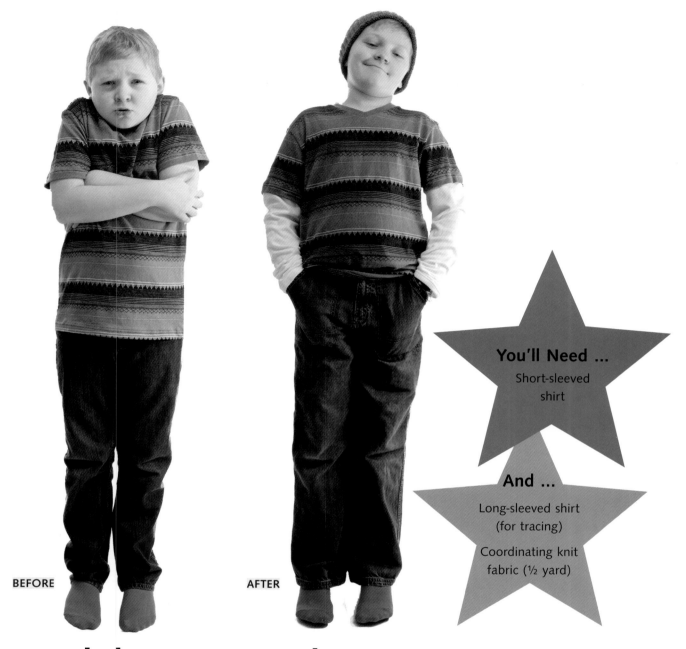

BEFORE

AFTER

Add Long Sleeves

Add warmth to a short-sleeved shirt and get a layered look without the bulk by adding quick sleeves. If it still fits in the warmer season, just pull out the stitches and enjoy short sleeves again!

1. Place a long sleeve flat on the knit fabric on a lengthwise fold. Trace around the sleeve with a fabric-marking pen, adding ½" to the side and 2" to the hem. Cut out along the marked lines. Cut another piece exactly the same for the second sleeve.

2. Lay a sleeve piece down next to the short-sleeved shirt to make sure the widths match up. The long-sleeve piece (folded) should be ½" wider than the short sleeve. Repeat for the second sleeve.

3. Fold the sleeve in half lengthwise with right sides facing. Pin and sew the seam.

4. Hem the bottom of the new sleeve with 2 rows of stitching. Use a strip of stabilizer inside the hem if desired.

5. Put the top of the long sleeve inside the short sleeve opening, with right sides facing up. Match the underarm seams and pin. Check the finished length of the sleeve on your child. **E**

6. Sew the sleeves together, being careful not to catch the body of the shirt in the seam. **F**

7. Repeat Steps 3–6 for the second sleeve.

TIP For a super-easy version, cut off the legs from some too-small knit pajama pants and use them as sleeves!

Tyler, who do you think should be president? "My grandpa, because he is smart and knows what to do."

BEFORE

AFTER

Shortening Sleeves— Three Ways

Shortening sleeves is one of the easiest refashions you can do. Go from winter length to summer sleeves three different ways!

Option 1: Rolled Edge

1. Cut the sleeves off 1″ below the desired finished length.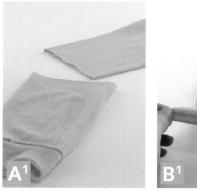

2. Gently stretch the cut edge of the sleeves to create a rolled edge.

3. Tack the rolled edge in place with a needle and thread by sewing an X at the underarm and the shoulder edges of the sleeves. Sew short lines every inch or so in between the X's.

Option 2: Folded Edge

1. Cut the sleeves off 2″ below the desired finished length.

2. Fold the edge up 1″ and iron; then fold up another 1″. Pin in place.

3. Sew 2 parallel rows of straight stitches, or use a double needle to create a professional-looking hem. If you need more stretch in the sleeves, use a zigzag stitch.

Option 3: Stripes

1. Cut off the sleeves at the desired finished length. Measure the sleeve opening all around.

2. Cut 2 strips of contrasting knit with the length equal to the sleeve opening plus 1″. Cut the bottom strip the width of the desired finished trim (3″–4″). Cut the top strip 1″ narrower.

3. Lay the narrower strip on top of the wider strip, right sides facing up. There should be ½″ of the bottom strip visible on the long sides of the top strip. Fold the strips in half crosswise, right sides facing. Pin and sew the short ends together. Turn right side out.

4. Pin the double strip to the sleeves, with the seams matching and right sides facing up. Sew along the top and bottom edges of the top strip.

ANOTHER FIX-IT OPTION

- Bow-Neck Tank (page 114)

Dylan, what is the hardest thing you've ever done?
"Staying away from my baby brother."

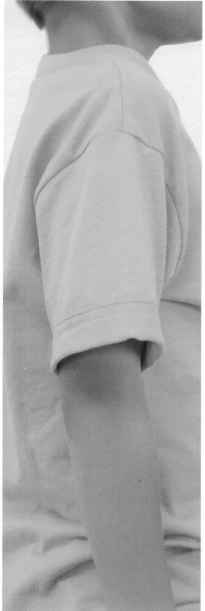

You'll Need ...
Long-sleeved T-shirt
or blouse

BEFORE

AFTER

Bow-Neck Tank

Another great way to go from winter to summer is to use long sleeves to create a sweet bow accent around the neckline. It looks adorable, and no one will guess that you did it yourself!

1. Cut off the sleeves from the T-shirt or blouse about 1″ from the armholes.

2. Cut 2 strips from each sleeve in matching widths. The strips should be as wide and as long as possible. Sew the strip ends together with right sides facing to make a single long strip.

3. Fold the strip in half lengthwise. Pin together on the long edge and sew.

4. Turn the strip inside out using the safety pin technique in Turning a Fabric Tube (page 16). Fold the ends toward the inside of the strip and sew closed.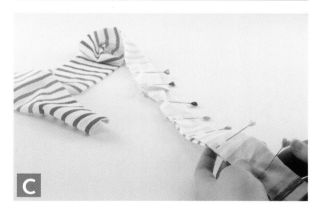

5. Fold the strip in half crosswise to find the midpoint. Pin the midpoint of the strip to the center back of the neckline. Continue pinning around the neckline, leaving a few inches open in the front. Sew on, leaving the ends of the strip loose for tying.

6. Turn the edges of the armhole under twice, ½″ per fold, and hem. The top edge of the hem should match up with the existing armhole seam. F

TIP Want to make the shirt but keep the sleeves? Simply use a coordinating fabric for the bow neck!

ANOTHER FIX-IT OPTION

- Shortening Sleeves–Three Ways (page 110)

Paige, *what are you super good at? "Crafts."*

BEFORE

AFTER

You'll Need ...

T-shirt with out-of-season or undesirable design

White or coordinating knit fabric, prewashed

And ...

Ribbon or other decorative trim

Acrylic paint and paintbrush, or fabric pens

Work-of-Art Shirt
(Replacing a Design)

Maybe it's that cute little Easter Bunny shirt you bought that finally fit him in June. Or maybe it's that shirt with the skull and crossbones that your little princess refuses to wear. No problem! Replace any embellishment with your child's own work of art for a shirt he or she will be proud to put on!

1. Cut a large square or rectangle out of the shirt, removing the out-of-season design.

2. Cut a piece of the knit fabric about 1″ larger on each side than the piece you cut out of the shirt. Let your child decorate the knit fabric with paint or fabric markers. Set the paint following the instructions in Freezer-Paper Stenciling (page 15).

3. Pin the decorated square to the right side of the shirtfront, covering the cut-out area on all sides. Sew together with a zigzag stitch. Be sure the design is facing outward.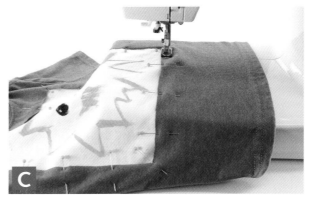

4. Make a "frame" for the artwork by sewing on ribbon, lace, rickrack, or other decorative trimming on the right side of the shirt front.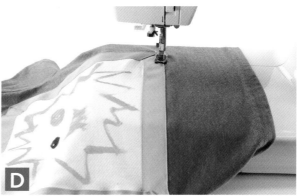

TIP If needed, shorten the sleeves using one of the sleeve-shortening techniques (Shortening Sleeves— Three Ways, page 110).

TIP If your child isn't the artistic type, let him or her pick out a fun cotton print to be framed on the shirt.

ANOTHER FIX-IT OPTION

- Ruffle-Panel Shirt (page 79)
- T-Shirt Transplant (page 92)

Skylar, *what do you want for your next birthday? "Cake."*

BEFORE

AFTER

Coat to Cropped Jacket

My daughter once had an adorable little plaid trench coat that I simply could not let go when she grew out of it. So I trimmed a little fabric from the bottom and the arms, and she wore her cute little "cropped jacket" for another full year!

1. Cut the cuffs off the sleeves, leaving ½″ of fabric above the cuffs.

2. Trim the sleeves to the desired length plus a ½″ seam allowance, keeping in mind the length of the cuff you will add back on. **B**

3. Pin the sleeve cuffs back onto the jacket with right sides facing and raw edges flush. Sew together as close to the cuffs' seams as possible. **C**

4. Sew along the raw edges with a zigzag stitch, or trim with pinking shears, to prevent fraying. **D**

TIP If you'd like to shorten the body of the jacket as well, simply cut off the bottom 2″ below the desired length and then fold the edge under 1″, then another 1″, and sew.

OTHER FIX-IT OPTIONS

- Suddenly Longer Jacket (page 58)
- Coat to Vest (page 61)

Paige, *what is your favorite thing to wear? "Hearts!"*

BEFORE

AFTER

You'll Need ...

Shorts

Coordinating fabric, or legs from too-small pants

And ...

Stencil

Acrylic paint and paintbrush

Shorts to Pants

Do his favorite shorts still fit when summer ends? Turn them into pants by adding coordinating fabric or the cut-off legs of a pair of pants that have gotten too small.

1. Use a purchased stencil or your own freezer-paper stencil to add designs to the shorts in a color that matches the fabric (see Freezer-Paper Stenciling, page 15). **A**

2. Measure the leg openings of the shorts. Cut 2 rectangles of coordinating fabric, with the width equal to the leg opening plus 1″ and the length equal to the desired added length plus 3″. **B**

3. Fold the fabric in half lengthwise with right sides facing. Pin and sew the side seam. Repeat for the other leg piece. **C**

4. Hem the top and bottom of each leg piece with a ½″ double-fold hem. Turn the pieces right side out. **D**

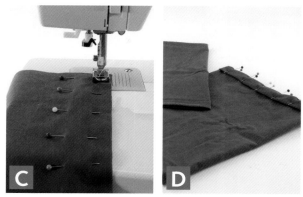

5. With the added leg piece inside the leg opening of the shorts, hand stitch the leg piece to the shorts' original hem. Repeat for the other pant leg. **E**

ANOTHER FIX-IT OPTION

- Shorts to Lounge Pants (page 124)

BEFORE

AFTER

You'll Need ...
Knit shorts

Coordinating strips
of knit fabric
(½–1 yard total)

Shorts to Lounge Pants

Turn warm-weather shorts into cold-weather lounge pants
with a fun twist using knit remnants.

1. Measure around the leg openings of the shorts.

2. Cut 2 knit rectangles with the length equal to the leg opening plus 1″ and the width about 4″. **B**

3. Sew the short ends of each rectangle together, right sides facing, to make 2 circles. **C**

4. With right sides facing and side seams matching, pin and sew the new layers to the leg openings. Use a ½″ strip of stabilizer along the seamline if desired. **D**

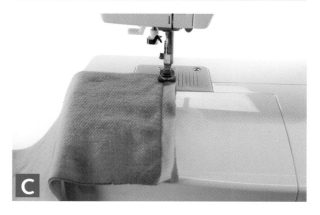

5. Repeat Steps 1–4 for as many layers as you need. Hem the bottom of the last layer.

TIPS Make the added layers as long or short as you'd like for different color-block looks. Or use the shirring technique (page 16) on the bottom of the legs.

For a less loungy but cute look, use monotone layers and nonknit fabrics.

OTHER FIX-IT OPTIONS

- Shorts to Skort (page 127)

- Shorts to Pants (page 122)

- Wear with tights or leggings (Restyling Ideas, page 129)

Lexi, *who would you most like to meet? "A real princess, not just a girl dressed up."*

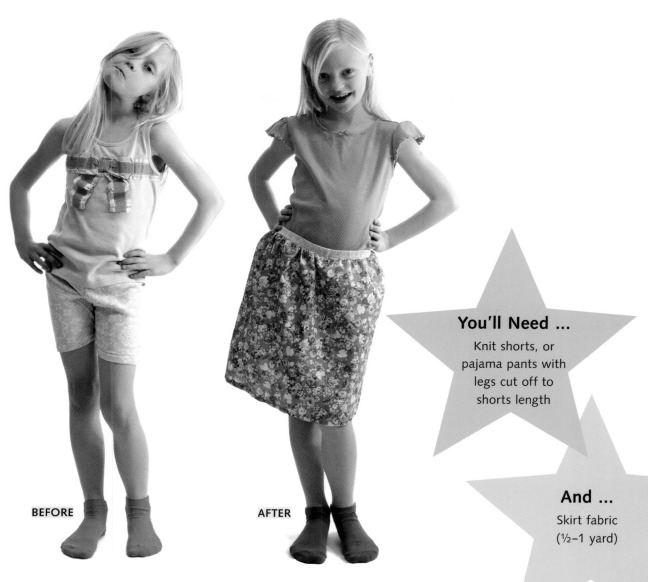

BEFORE

AFTER

Shorts to Skort

Paige loves wearing skirts, but she doesn't love hearing "Honey, put your skirt down" a hundred times a day. That's why I adore making these skorts out of knit shorts. The process is so quick that you can make several in one afternoon!

1. Measure the pants waistband all around. Cut a rectangular skirt piece with the width equal to twice the pants' waistband measurement, plus 1˝. The length should be the desired finished length plus 2˝.

2. Fold lengthwise and sew the sides of the skirt piece together with right sides facing. Hem the bottom edge with a 1˝ single-fold hem. **B**

3. Using the ruffling technique (see Sewing a Ruffle, page 11), gather the top edge of the skirt piece until it is the same size as the waistband. **C**

4. Pin the skirt piece upside down just below the waistband, with right sides facing. **D**

5. Sew together with a narrow zigzag stitch. **E**

TIP Make a multilayered version by making two skirt pieces in different lengths and sewing them onto the shorts together.

OTHER FIX-IT OPTIONS

- Shorts to Lounge Pants (page 124)
- PJ Pants to Bubble Skirt (page 35)

BONUS

Restyling Ideas

Altering clothes is so much fun. But sometimes you can wear clothes out of season with no alterations at all. Use your imagination (and your child's imagination, too!) to find new combinations and blend the lines between summer and winter.

Turn a dress into a tunic, or even a shirt, just by pairing it with skinny pants.

Roll up long pants into capris.

Let them wear tights under their shorts.

Brighten up dark colors with light, summery accessories.

Layer tanks over sleeved shirts.

Paige, *what is your favorite kind of sandwich? "Dairy-free grilled cheese."*

IF ALL ELSE FAILS—
ACCESSORIZE!

Has your child ever had a garment that was so far gone you didn't even want to donate it? Surely there isn't any hope for those worn-out, faded pajama pants. Or is there? One of the great things about clothing is that even when it seems to be useless for wear, the fabric can still be used—even if it's only a scrap to make a hair clip.

BEFORE

AFTER

You'll Need ...

Stained and too-small
T-shirt or tights

½˝-wide elastic

T-Shirt Headband

A great way to use T-shirts or tights that have seen better days is by braiding strips into a sweet headband. Let your girls choose wide strips for a bigger braid or narrow strips for a subtler look.

1. Cut 3 long strips, each 2″–4″ wide, from the front or back of the T-shirt.

2. Stretch each strip so that the edges roll in slightly. Pin an end of each strip onto a pincushion. **B**

3. Braid the strips all the way down. Trim so that the braid fits snugly around your child's head, with a 3″ gap between the ends. Pin each end to secure it. **C**

4. Sew an end of the braid to a 3″–4″ piece of elastic. Pin the other end to the elastic and check the fit. Sew. **D**

5. Wrap a small scrap of knit around the elastic at each end where it joins the braid. Sew on. **E**

TIP Try with different colors of knit scraps or rows of multiple smaller braids for a different look.

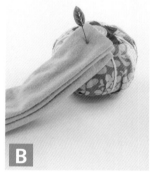

OTHER FIX-IT OPTIONS

- Poppy Hair Clips (page 146)

- Poppies on the Poppy-Scattered Shirt (page 85)

- Butterflies on the Butterfly Cutout Shirt (page 83)

- Sweater Belt (page 132)

Alyssa, *what is your favorite thing in the world? "My baby brother, 'Cheekers.'"*

BEFORE

AFTER

You'll Need ...
Too-small or damaged
lightweight sweater

1″ D-rings (set of 2)

Sweater Belt

A sweater that is too small or worn out can find
new purpose as a great-looking girl's or boy's belt.

1. Cut a piece from the bottom or middle of the sweater that is about 4″ wide, and snip a side open to form a strip. Cut pieces from the sleeves in the same way if additional belt length is needed. **A**

2. If you are working with a very small sweater, it may be necessary to cut multiple strips. Then sew them end-to-end, with right sides facing, to make a single long strip. **B**

3. Fold the strip in half lengthwise with right sides facing, and serge or sew with a zigzag stitch. Let the strip stretch naturally as you sew. **C**

4. Turn right side out using the safety pin technique in Turning a Fabric Tube (page 16). Then turn the ends under and sew closed. **D**

5. Loop an end through both D-rings and fold back over the straight edge of the rings. Sew in place. **E**

TIP Other pieces of clothing will work for this belt, too—T-shirts, old dresses, even colored jeans!

Brayden, *if you were an animal, you'd be: "A shark."*

OTHER FIX-IT OPTIONS

- Arm or Leg Warmers (page 142)

- Sweater Beanie (page 152)

BEFORE

AFTER

You'll Need ...
Collar from a too-small or damaged shirt or dress

And ...
½″-wide satin ribbon (about 20″)

Sequined Collar

There is nothing sweeter than a Peter Pan collar. Add sequins or lace trim to the collar of an outgrown shirt for a precious accessory that can be worn with almost any outfit.

1. Cut the collar off as close to the seam as possible. Serge or zigzag stitch the raw edge, or enclose it in bias tape.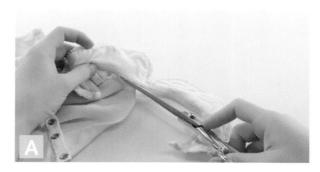

2. Stitch or hot glue sequins, lace, or other decorative trim to the right side of the collar. Start at the outside edge and move inward. Turn under the ends of the trim.

3. Cut 2 pieces of satin ribbon 10″ each and hem both ends of each piece. Sew a ribbon to the back of each end of the collar.

Kayla, what makes you upset? "When people are mean at me."

ANOTHER FIX-IT OPTION

- Bib-Front Shirt (page 100)

BEFORE

AFTER

You'll Need ...

Old pair of pants

Fleece fabric
60˝ wide (½ yard)

Scarf with Pockets

Remove the pockets from unusable pants and sew them
to a fleece scarf for a unique accessory that keeps him
(or her!) toasty warm.

1. Cut 2 strips of fleece 8″ wide, across the full width of the fabric.

2. Cut the pockets off the pants, leaving 1″ around the sides and bottom. Pin a pocket on each end of a fleece strip. Position the pockets at a comfortable height for your child.

3. Sew the pockets to the scarf piece with the raw edges tucked neatly underneath.

4. Lay the other strip of fleece on top of the first piece with right sides facing. Pin the sides, leaving the ends open.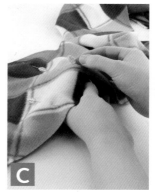

5. Sew along the pinned edges and turn right side out.

6. Turn the edges of each end to the inside of the scarf and sew closed.

OTHER FIX-IT OPTIONS

- Pockets for Pants to Cargo Shorts (page 33)
- Legs for Shorts to Pants (page 122)

Tyler, *if you were an animal, you'd be: "A cat."*

You'll Need ...

Old dress, T-shirt, or other garment

Beads, or ¾" foam beads

BEFORE   AFTER

Covered Bead Necklace

Her favorite dress that she wants to wear every day has been through the wringer. When it's too small (and covered in stains), try turning it into this super-cute necklace that she can wear as long as she wants! She'll love helping with the process, too.

1. Cut several 3½"-wide strips and sew the ends together to make a strip 70" long. **A**

2. Fold the strip in half lengthwise and sew a seam on the long side. **B**

3. Turn right side out using the safety pin technique (see Turning a Fabric Tube, page 16). **C**

4. Tie a knot in the fabric 12" from the end. **D**

5. Put in a bead and slide it to the bottom, next to the knot. Tie another knot right next to the bead. **E**

6. Repeat Step 5 until you have about 13 beads. Trim the fabric to leave 12" after the last knot. Turn the ends to the inside of the tube and sew closed. **F**

TIP Stitch on a flower embellishment using the poppy flower pattern (see Patterns, page 158) or the circle flower from the No-Sew Flower Sash (page 154).

OTHER FIX-IT OPTIONS

- Easy-On Infinity Scarf (page 150)
- As-Long-as-You-Like Skirt (page 56)
- Overall Overhaul (page 53)

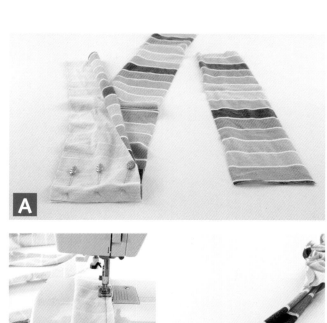

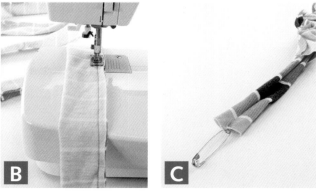

BEFORE

AFTER

You'll need ...
Old shirt or pajamas,
or other fabric

½"-wide elastic

Retro Tie

Vintage-style ties look adorable on boys or girls.
Make your own using shirt sleeves or even a pair
of waffle-knit pajama pants.

1. Cut a 5″ × 10″ rectangle and a 3″ × 7″ rectangle from the sleeves of an old garment. (These dimensions are good for a medium-sized tie.) Cut 11″ of elastic.

2. Gather a long side of the 7″ rectangle using the ruffling technique (see Sewing a Ruffle, page 11) until it is 5″ wide. Pin to the 5″ side of the 5″ × 10″ rectangle with right sides facing. **B**

3. Sew together. **C**

4. Fold the tie in half lengthwise and sew all the way down the side. **D**

5. Turn it right side out and iron flat with the seam centered on the back. **E**

6. Turn the top and bottom edges under and sew closed using the slip-stitch technique (page 13). Sew the ends of the elastic together and stitch to the back of the tie. **F**

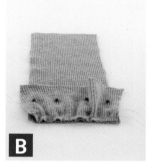

OTHER FIX-IT OPTIONS

- T-Shirt Shoelaces (page 144)
- Butterfly Cutout Shirt (page 83)

Skylar, *what is the prettiest color ever? "Orange."*

You'll Need ...

Old sweater

Elastic thread

BEFORE

AFTER

Arm or Leg Warmers

Every year my daughter and I make a new pair of leg warmers from the sleeves of last year's cuddly sweater. They're quick and fun, and I can't get enough of her cute little legs in them!

1. Cut the sleeves off the sweater just below the underarms.

2. Turn the top edges under and sew a row using the shirring technique (page 16).

3. Shirr 3 or 4 more rows.

4. Stitch on buttons or get creative with flowers or other embellishments!

TIP Have her wear them peeking out from a pair of boots, or even on her arms.

Sarah, if you were an animal, you'd be: "A butterfly."

OTHER FIX-IT OPTIONS

- Sweater Beanie (page 152)

- Sweater Belt (page 132)

- Retro Tie (page 140)— (if the sweater is lightweight)

BEFORE

AFTER

T-Shirt Shoelaces

Cut a trash-worthy tee into strips to make awesome
shoelaces. Your kids will love having their own
homemade laces, and you'll love getting use out of
something you would have thrown away.

1. Cut several long 1½"-wide strips from the pajamas. Cut the strips as long as possible.

2. Sew the ends of the strips together to make 2 strips that are at least 30" long.

3. Gently stretch each strip lengthwise. If the edges of the strips curl, continue to Step 5.

4. If the strips don't curl on the edges, fold each strip in half lengthwise with wrong sides facing and serge or zigzag the full length.

5. Wrap ½" sections of clear packing tape tightly around each end several times.

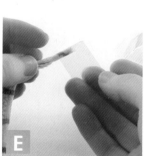

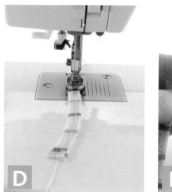

OTHER FIX-IT OPTIONS

- T-Shirt Headband (page 130)
- Faux Plaid Shirt (page 88)

Brayden, *what makes you upset? "Having to listen."*

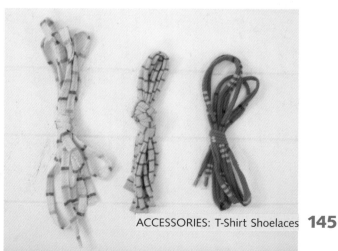

BEFORE

AFTER

Poppy Hair Clips

These hair clips are proof that even the tiniest scraps of clothing can be useful. You can also put the poppies on pins, on headbands, or even on the side of a purse or pillow.

1. Trace large, medium, and small poppy patterns (see Patterns, page 158) onto paper or template plastic. Trace the template designs onto the fabric with a fabric-marking pen. You'll need a piece of each size for the flower.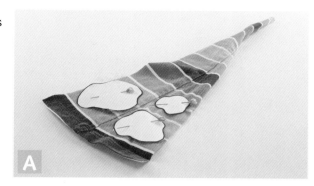

2. Lay the petals on top of each other, with the smallest petal on top, and stitch together with an X in the middle.

3. Use a hot glue gun to glue the ribbon to an alligator clip or barrette.

4. Glue the poppy flower to the top of the clip.

OTHER FIX-IT OPTIONS

Use scraps for:

- Butterfly Cutout Shirt (page 83)
- No-Sew Flower Sash (page 154)
- Polka-Dot Sweater Patches (page 90)

TIPS

- Try stitching a bead or button to the center of the flower.
- Use the circle flower technique from the No-Sew Flower Sash (page 154) to add a different flower.
- Glue multiple poppies to a plastic headband.

Lexi, *how many people are in the world?* *"200–600 million-thousand."*

BEFORE

AFTER

Bow Tie

Before throwing away a ragged old button-up, snip off the collar and whip it into a darling little gentleman's bow tie!

1. Cut the collar off the shirt, cutting as close to the seam as possible. **A**

2. Turn the raw edges under and sew the opening closed. **B**

3. Fold the collar in a Z shape, with the 2 bottom layers sticking out slightly more than the top layer, and pin in place. **C**

4. Cut a 1½″ × 3″ rectangle from the sleeve cuff. Turn the raw edges under and sew closed. **D**

5. Fold the small cuff piece in half lengthwise and wrap it snugly around the tie to make a loop. Hand stitch or glue on. **E**

6. Cut an 11″ piece of elastic. Slip the elastic through the back of the tie loop and stitch the ends together. **F**

7. If the shirt collar has buttonholes, cover the buttonhole in front with a little felt heart or "kiss." **G**

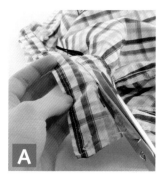
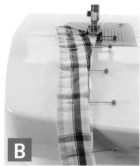
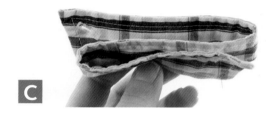

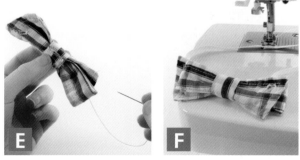

Brayden, where would you like to go on vacation? "Grandma's house."

BEFORE

AFTER

Easy-On Infinity Scarf

When my daughter was young, she could never keep a scarf on. With a hook-and-loop tape closure on the back, this dress-turned-scarf stays on and stays cute.

1. Remove the waistband or bodice and cut up the back of the skirt piece from the waist to the hem to make a large rectangle.  A

2. Cut the rectangle in half lengthwise to make 2 rectangles, and hem the long sides. B

3. Lay the 2 pieces in an X shape.  C

4. Bring both ends of a scarf piece together with the edges flush. Fold both edges over together and hem (double-check the length before hemming). Repeat for the other scarf piece. You'll have 2 interlocking circles of fabric.  D

5. Fold each end into thirds lengthwise and pin. Sew the ends along the pinned edge. 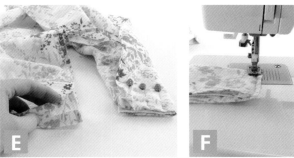 E F

6. Sew a few inches of hook-and-loop tape to each end of the scarf. G

TIP This project works best with lightweight fabrics such as cotton, silk blends, or lightweight flannel.

OTHER FIX-IT OPTIONS

- Shorts to Skort (page 127)
- PJ Pants to Bubble Skirt (page 35)

Sarah, *is it hard to sew clothes?* "Nope, it's easy peasy lemon squeezy."

BEFORE

AFTER

Sweater Beanie

Some see a too-small sweater, but we see a
too-cute hat! Use felt or fleece to add crazy
eyebrows or anything else you can think up.

1. Measure around your child's head. At the bottom edge of the sweater, measure a distance equal to half your child's head circumference, plus 1″. With the measured edge as a base, cut a dome shape through both layers of the sweater. The height of the dome should be about the same as the length of the base.

2. Pin the 2 pieces together with right sides facing, leaving the bottom edge open. **B**

3. Serge or zigzag around the pinned edges to make a ½″ seam. Turn right side out. **C**

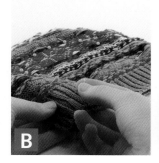 

For Eyebrow Variation: Cut 2 rectangles of felt (approximately 1″ × 2½″) and snip out tiny triangles around all the sides. Sew the rectangles to the front of the hat, about 1″ from the bottom. **D**

For Earflap Variation: Cut 2 smaller dome shapes for each earflap, allowing ½″ all around for seams. Follow Steps 2 and 3 to complete the flaps. Pin and sew to the inside of the bottom of the hat on each side. **E**

OTHER FIX-IT OPTIONS

- Sweater Belt (page 132)
- Arm or Leg Warmers (page 142)

Elijah, *what is your favorite color? "Blue."*

BEFORE

AFTER

No-Sew Flower Sash

This precious flower sash is my favorite way to use small scraps. It's easy to customize: one flower or many, centered or off-center, one fabric or several different fabrics.

1. Cut 1 felt circle 1½″ in diameter and 8 fabric circles 3″ in diameter.

2. Fold 4 fabric circles in half and then in half again. Snip off the corners. **B**

TIP If your fabric frays easily, add a bit of antifray product to the edges of each circle before folding.

3. Hot glue the 4 flower petals to the edges of the felt circle. **C**

4. Repeat Step 2 for the other 4 circles and then glue them to the center of the felt circle. **D**

5. Repeat Steps 1–4 for each flower. **E**

6. Cut a piece of ribbon long enough to tie as a belt, and trim each end at a 45° angle. Hot glue flowers to the center front. **F**

TIP Make a sparkly version by using stretchy sequin trim with two snap closures sewn to the ends.

OTHER FIX-IT OPTIONS

Use scraps for:

- Poppy Hair Clips (page 146)
- Poppy-Scattered Shirt (page 85)
- Butterfly Cutout Shirt (page 83)

PATTERNS

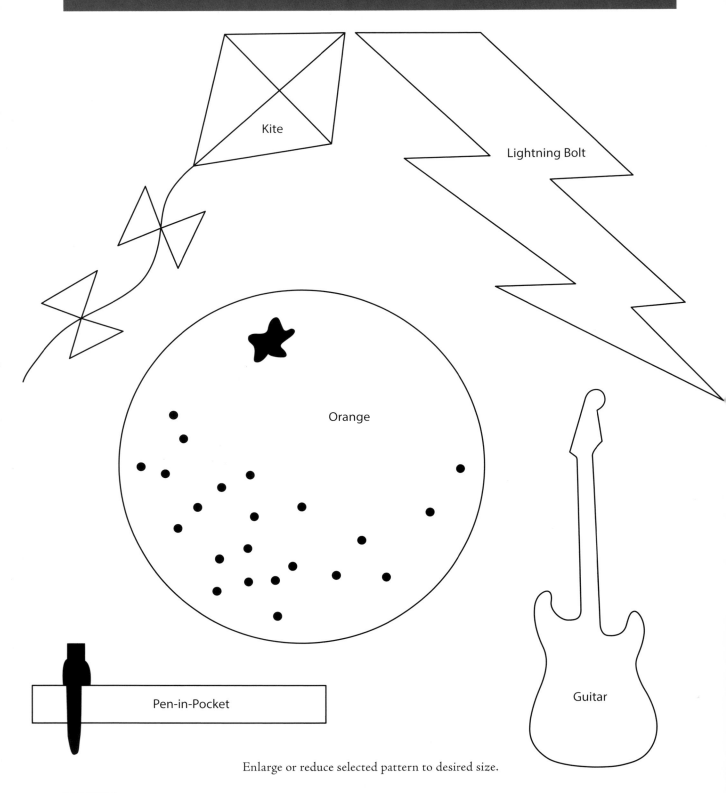

Kite

Lightning Bolt

Orange

Guitar

Pen-in-Pocket

Enlarge or reduce selected pattern to desired size.

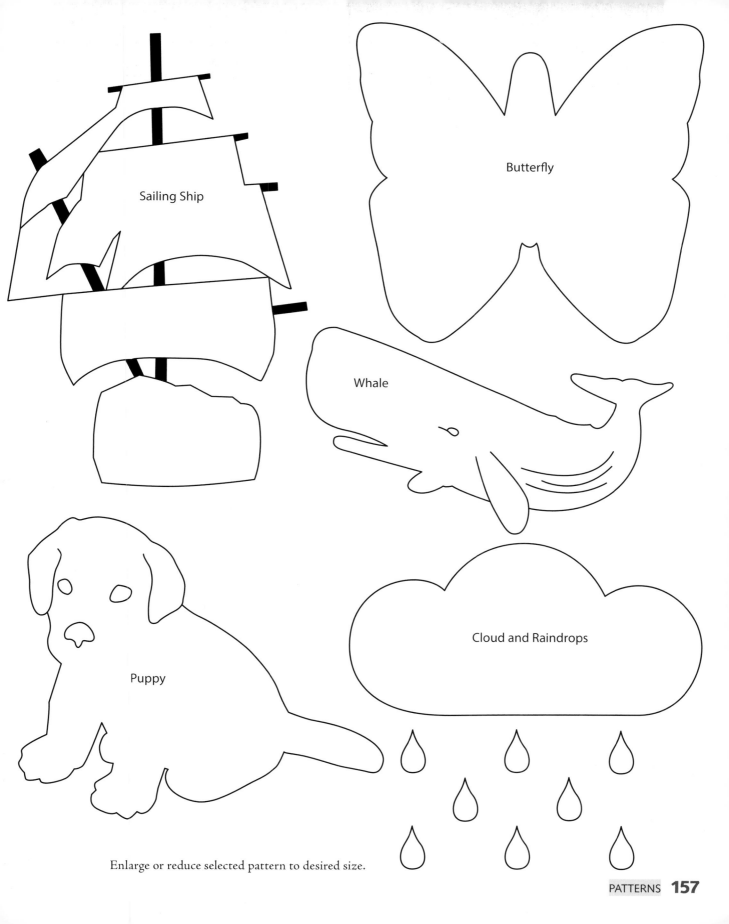

Sailing Ship

Butterfly

Whale

Puppy

Cloud and Raindrops

Enlarge or reduce selected pattern to desired size.

Large Poppy

Small Poppy

Medium Poppy

Airplane

Star

Heart

Enlarge or reduce selected pattern to desired size.